Meditations to Enhance Your Enlightenment

12 Steps to a Lightness of Being

Sarah Goddard Neves

12 Steps to a Lightness of Being

Meditations to Enhance Your Enlightenment

Sarah Goddard Neves

Light Technology Publishing

For more information about special discounts for bulk purchases, please contact Light Technology Publishing Special Sales at 1-800-450-0985 or publishing@LightTechnology.net

Cover artwork: Archangel Chamuel's Loving Light
Lightworks Art by Goldenlight • www.thegoldenlightchannel.com

* * *

ISBN-13: 978-1-891824-99-9

Light Technology Publishing

Light Technology Publishing, LLC
Phone: 800-450-0985
928-526-1345
Fax: 928-714-1132
PO Box 3540
Flagstaff, AZ 86003
www.LightTechnology.com

Contents

indicates recorded meditation on CDs

How to Use This Book

It may seem a little unusual to tell someone how to read a book, but for this one, I feel it is necessary. Today we live in a world where doing things quickly seems to be the best way, and that can even apply to reaching enlightenment! Therefore, if you want to read this book from front to back in a weekend, then I really can't stop you. However, this unique book has been designed as if you were taking a very special spiritual development course in the comfort of your own home. Through its wisdom and visualizations, *12 Steps to a Lightness of Being* will gradually but surely lift your vibration and awaken you. Therefore, to get the most out of it, decide now not to rush it but to read it slowly. Take as long as you need on each step before moving on to the next. Commit to doing each meditation or visualization, giving yourself some quiet, undisturbed time to do this, and recall your meditation experiences and insights afterward. By doing so, you will get the most out of reading this book.

In the first step of *12 Steps to a Lightness of Being*, you will learn to do a particular meditation called "meditation on the light." As this meditation is fundamental to helping you raise your vibration and bring in important insights, it is suggested that you practice the meditation on the light as often as you can while reading the book, along with doing the other visualizations.

It is best not to start or mix any other spiritual development courses or modalities until you have finished this book. Each step of *12 Steps to a Lightness of Being* is a supportive tool that you are learning, and these steps — or tools — can be used to assist you as you continue to grow in the future. After finishing the book, feel free to use any of the steps or the visualizations whenever you feel you need clarity, to help you overcome blocks, or for inspiration and insight.

Lastly, if there is anything that you read that does not ring true for you or does not feel right to you, then please feel free to skip it and follow what does. I sincerely hope that you find the wisdom, techniques, and visualizations personally awakening and empowering and that you enjoy reading and becoming a lightness of being.

—Sarah Goddard Neves

Acknowledgments

First and foremost, I want to thank Supreme Spirit for my life and for all the inspiration that came through me to write this book. I would also like to thank my spiritual masters and the many other great ones and saints that also communicate with me with guidance and support and who always hold the cosmic lantern of wisdom, love, and light to show me the way. I would also like to thank two very special people in my life who truly know who I am: my husband Rui, who loves me deeply and who supported me and spurred me on to write this book, and my daughter Chloe, who brings me so much joy and love.

Dedication

This book is for all those who are choosing to grow spiritually and lighten up, for without you soul seekers out there, this book would have never been written.

Step 1
Meditation on the Light

Meditation is the foundation for spiritual awakening. It is through the practice of meditation that soulful states like inner peace, wisdom, and joy can be found within, which when experienced, can positively affect the way you live your life. And if you want to discover more about who you truly are and the nature of Supreme Spirit, meditation can be the key to assist you in achieving these goals. In this chapter, you will be looking at special forms of meditation to accelerate your spiritual growth to help bring about a lightness of being.

Whenever you are totally engaged and at one with what you are doing — for example, reading a book, painting a picture, or concentrating on performing a set of physical movements — you are, in fact, experiencing a type of meditation. While you are at one with any activity, time can seem to fly by as you soon forget your everyday concerns and duties, leaving you feeling more relaxed and at peace. So it could be true to say that most of you have probably experienced the benefits of meditation in some way or another.

Here you will be looking at the benefits of seated meditation focusing on the divine light, the image of Supreme Spirit. If you direct your intent and familiarize yourself with the holy light found at the area of your third eye (situated between your eyebrows in the center of your forehead), your vibration will begin to rise. It is through meditating on this area that you will make a stronger connection to your intuition to reveal wisdom and guidance on your highest good and to realize more about who you truly are. And with regular practice, over time it can cause you to merge with and experience the love and bliss of Supreme Spirit. Therefore, this form of meditation is extremely effective to help you evolve spiritually.

Getting Started

Prepare Yourself for Meditation

Nowadays, most of us have timetables busy with work, family, and home commitments to juggle. Nevertheless, when it comes to meditation, you will need to make some time in the day to do it. You may think of doing other things that seem more important, yet if you truly want to progress spiritually, meditation is a must.

Just like taking up a new form of exercise, it is best to start meditating little by little, steadily increasing your time. At first, start with just ten to fifteen minutes. Then go on to meditate for longer periods, gradually building up to half an hour — or more if you have the time. In the early hours of the morning or at night before you go to bed are both good times to meditate, but to be honest, any time of the day is just fine.

Attune Yourself to a Lightness of Being

All who have this book in their hands have been asking for it. That's why it has been written. Those of you who are already sensitive may have felt the lightness of being energy wash over you days before or just after you bought this book. That is a sure sign that you have already attuned yourself to this wonderful energy. However, for those of you who haven't consciously felt it yet and for those who want to intentionally align yourselves to it, here is an attunement to get you started.

- *Go somewhere quiet where you will be undisturbed.*
- *Take a few deep breathes.*
- *Place your left hand on the book (which is probably now open), and place your right hand over your heart.*
- *Now close your eyes, and let the feeling of a lightness of being flow through you for a few minutes.*

- *When you are ready, open your eyes.*
- *Relax for fifteen minutes or so.*

Congratulations! Whether you felt the special energy here or not, you have been successfully attuned and are ready to begin.

Creating a Sacred Space

You may like to give yourself a special space to carry out your meditations, although this is not a prerequisite. A corner of the room will do, or if you are lucky enough, you may have a whole room that you can dedicate to this practice. Most importantly, your meditation environment should be isolated, free from disturbing noises and intrusion. Keep this space clean and tidy to reflect your state of mind, decorating it with uplifting colors and white. Some of you might like to make an altar where you can sit and meditate. This can be decorated with photographs of enlightened gurus, spiritual teachers, and saints you feel you have a real affinity to. (You will discover more about who your special spiritual teachers are in step 3). Ornaments and symbols that represent Supreme Spirit, such as white candles, can evoke an uplifting and protective ambiance. Incense is great too, as the smoke helps to clear the space for deep meditation. If you need to wrap a blanket around you while meditating, make sure it is made with natural fibers of either wool or silk that are known to help intensify your awareness and repel certain earth currents.

Position and Posture

For those of you supple enough, sit cross-legged on the floor on a couple of thick, firm cushions to lift your seat off the ground. This will help keep your back relaxed and comfortable while you meditate in this position. For those of you who are less agile, sitting in a straight-backed chair with both feet flat on the ground will do the trick.

Your back should always be straight while meditating, as if there is a vertical line running from the bottom to the top of your spine, yet the rest of your body will feel relaxed. Your chin should be positioned just slightly in toward your chest and your shoulders relaxed. Relax your arms, careful not to let them cling to the sides of your body, and turn your palms upward, placing your right hand in your left palm (or vice versa if you are left-handed). Then allow your thumbs to touch. Most people like to close their eyes while meditating, but if you prefer, you may keep them open with your eyelids softened as if half-opened. You are now ready to meditate.

Breathing Technique: Calm the Mind

This is a breathing technique used to help you quiet your mind before meditating on the light. It will assist you in letting go of troubling thoughts and concerns to feel more calm and centered. It is especially recommended for those of you who are beginners to meditation and initially find it difficult to be in the moment, easily becoming sidetracked by your thoughts while meditating.

- *Go to a quiet place or room where you will be undisturbed and sit in the most comfortable meditation position and posture for you of those suggested.*
- *Close your eyes or keep them open with your eyelids relaxed.*

Now you are ready to practice calming the mind.

- *As you breathe in, imagine your breath is moving up from the bottom of your spine to the top of your head at the area of your crown.*
- *Hold your breath at the top of your head.*
- *Now breathe out, imagining that your breath is moving back down the front of your body, mirroring the line of your spine, until it reaches the bottom of your spine again.*

The aim here is to breathe in, hold, and breathe out for the same length of time. For example, breathe in for a count of ten, hold your breath for a count of ten, and breathe out for a count of ten. Find a number that you can do evenly and comfortably.

Let's practice this breathing technique together.

- *Continue to concentrate breathing this way at least six to twelve times or until your mind and emotions feel calmer.*

Now you are ready to practice the focus of light meditation.

Meditation: a Focus of Light

For those of you who are beginners to meditation, practice the breathing technique to calm the mind for a while first. For those of you who are more experienced at meditating, you might like to go straight into this meditation. So let's begin.

- *Breathe normally now. If necessary, adjust your meditation posture so that you are sitting upright with your spine straight and your shoulders relaxed.*
- *With your eyes closed, or if you prefer half-open, look up and out of your third eye, an area situated in the middle of your forehead between your eyebrows.*
- *Continue to look up and out of your third eye. It is from this area that you may see a bright light like a star or sun shining above you. If you do not see a light, do not worry or think that you are doing anything wrong. Just gently but surely keep looking up and out of this space.*
- *Know that as you connect with this higher space, you are being enveloped with divine light.*
- *Go with your experiences and acknowledge any special feelings or insights that you might have while you are meditating.*
- *Continue to meditate on this light for as long as you can. For beginners, start with ten to fifteen minutes, and then gradually lengthen the time if you so wish.*
- *When you are ready to finish, place your hands in prayer position, bow your head, and give thanks to the light of Supreme Spirit for blessing you today.*
- *Open your eyes, and come back into the room.*

Before continuing with your day, take some quiet time to contemplate your meditation experience.

Further Guidance

When you first concentrate on the Supreme Light, you may find it relaxes you so much that it can make you feel a bit sleepy. However, with regular practice, you will gradually get attuned to this high frequency and the drowsiness will subside.

It is not necessary to see the light at your third eye to know that you are making a higher connection to Spirit, so do not force yourself to see it. Relax. As you look out through your third eye (or brow chakra), you will instantly connect yourself to this higher space.

Remember that what you put in, you will get back multiplied. As you continue to meditate on the light, you will be raising your vibration and opening yourself up to many insights and positive spiritual experiences that you will not want to go without.

Sing Your Note

Meditating with sound is another effective practice that can bring about a sense of wholeness and balance. Simply expressing natural and harmonious sounds as a meditation will not only calm and center you but it can also have the profound effect of helping you overcome burdens and barriers to reveal your true power, allowing you to experience breakthroughs in blocked energy and tune into insights about your personal development from your higher self. Here you will use your instinct to know what sounds to make by trusting in whatever beautiful sounds you feel like making at the time.

All of you have your own unique sound that resonates and touches you deeply. Singing your sound or having harmonious sounds sung or played over you is powerfully balancing and healing, and it can help you get to the root of a problem that perhaps other holistic healing methods like massage or yoga may not be able to reach. Making comfortable, nice sounds can not only help balance and clear your aura, but can also increase your self-awareness and awaken you to act in ways that are for your highest good.

In ancient times, people knew how to deteriorate, regenerate, or reorganize their bodily cells through the power of sound. For example, Buddhist monks chant together and ring special bowls to harmonize their energy and spiritually awaken, and the Native Americans used song and dance to make it rain. The idea of using sound to help balance and clear your energy is gradually making a comeback. Regularly making beautiful sounds on your own or with others as a meditation will definitely leave you feeling uplifted. Some even find that they can reach states of bliss through singing, chanting, and toning together.

Chant the Word of Supreme Spirit

The sacred sound and word of Supreme Spirit is *Om* or *Aum*. Chanting *Om* out loud or mentally when meditating on the divine light can reinforce your connection to the Source.

As your vibration rises through meditation on the light, you may come to hear this ever-present sound of *Om* in the air. It can sound like a ringing or buzzing in the ears, similar to the sound you hear after listening to a loud rock concert. Alternatively, if you put your thumbs in your ears, you can hear *Om* like the roar of a nearby sea. All good comes from hearing this sacred sound, and chanting it will help raise your consciousness to unite with Supreme Spirit.

Meditation Increases Your Self-Awareness

Let us examine the problems with harboring a lot of unexpressed anger. Pent-up anger can negatively affect your state of mind and health. Firstly, your muscles become tense and your jaw tightens up through feeling angry. Then your body is flooded with stress chemicals and other metabolic changes occur, along with increases in your heart rate, blood pressure, and respiration. Energetically, your aura and chakras alter their harmonious flow, stopping the cosmic life force from coming into your body, which then depletes your energy and negatively changes the way your cells function. Over time, built-up anger can lead to more serious medical conditions such as skin disorders, ulcers, depression, and even heart attacks and strokes. In fact, an accumulation of any negative emotion can make you seriously ill, not to mention that when you are feeling negative, it is probably not the best time to make important decisions, as you may not be thinking straight.

It is true that anger can be a natural response because it tells us that we do not want or like something or perhaps that someone is taking advantage of us and can even help us get our power back when rising out of lower states like depression and grief. However, continuous unexpressed anger is not a natural state, and if held on to long enough, it could even lead you to mindlessly lash out and hurt another.

As you take steps to meditate on the light, your self-awareness of how you are thinking, feeling, and being in life increases. Growing spiritually means raising your vibration and being more of your intrinsic love, power, and light here in the physical, and it is through meditation that any lesser thoughts, feelings, or acts that are not in line with who you truly are will gradually be made conscious to you to positively transform. Any less-than-positive feeling, once you are made aware of it, is not to be fought against or gotten rid of; the aim is to unconditionally accept your lower emotion or feeling fully so it can move up in vibration. Many people on a spiritual path try to override this negativity or feel that they are bad or not spiritual enough because they feel the negativity, but unless you accept how you feel, you will get stuck and vibrate at that lower feeling — however low it is.

As your mind relaxes and your emotions calm in meditation, it gets easier for you to get into contact with your all-wise intuition that will enlighten you about your life. Thus, meditation can not only set you on a path of self-discovery and healing but will get you in line with your better nature.

Ask and Receive

Contemplating on the ever-bright light at the third eye gets you closer to Supreme Spirit, which can be a good time to pray and make your requests. See Supreme Spirit as your genie in a bottle, about to grant you your wishes and help you out like an ever-loving protector, provider, and friend. Then once you have made your supplication, continue to sit in peace and look out through your third eye to receive any related guidance that could help bring your wishes into fruition.

What type of loving and compassionate god would Supreme Spirit be to refuse your prayers? If you do not immediately receive what you ask for, you may tend to think that Supreme Spirit is deaf, has let you down, or perhaps just does not love you enough. However, the reason why you are not receiving could well lie within you. Negative underlying thoughts and beliefs about yourself and what you can have and create will hinder your ability to receive. For example, thoughts of unworthiness or of there not being enough — and that means anything, be it food, money, time, love, or something else that you have conjured up in your mind — to thoughts that "that sort of luck could never really happen to me" can create barriers, stopping you from receiving your good. What negative things do you say to yourself that block you from having your prayers answered?

Supreme Spirit works in mysterious ways. Perhaps you need time to prepare yourself to have what you are asking for, or maybe you need to let go of those things and thoughts that are no longer in line with your highest good before your prayer can be answered. Maybe you need to believe in yourself more or trust in Spirit to bring your plea forward, or perhaps what you are asking for is just not in your highest good to have. For example, a personal request to receive a new car may be withheld if, for some reason, you are not ready to have it or if having the car that you wish for may harm you in some way. Then you might have to wait while your higher self prepares you to have what you have asked for. To help make your wishes come true, be aware of and change your negative viewpoints into new and positive beliefs to help the cosmic love of Spirit stream through you to bring your pleas into fruition.

Alternatively, and more effectively, learn to request the essence of what you want. For instance, if you are calling for more love, light, friendship, abundance, or inner peace to come into your life, then that would be considered a soul request, a call for a feeling that you want to experience in life. Your soul can work with you more creatively to bring you unexpected gifts and opportunities for your highest good if you ask for the essence of what you want.

Be sincerely grateful when your prayers have been answered, as this will help attract more of Spirit's generosity to move into your life. Spiritual healers and spiritual masters practice saying thank you to the One before they are about to pray for something because of their complete faith and trust that all pleas to Supreme Spirit have already been answered and given. Yes, that's right — even *before* the asking! If you pacify your doubts and develop this immovable trust and faith, your days will be full of guidance and aid to help answer your prayers.

Release Your Spiritual Expectations

Spirit is never boring. Every time you meditate on the light, your experiences will most surely be different, but they will always be positive — and possibly enlightening. Apart from the advantage of feeling calmer from meditating, many times — especially if you are a beginner to meditation — you may feel as if you have not experienced anything specifically while meditating, yet the benefits will be found afterward as you go about your day with an increased feeling of inner peace, wakefulness, or energy.

In meditation, you might also receive guidance and insight about your life, or it could be sometime later in that day or a few days afterward that extra clarity on something important dawns on you. You may or may not see visions to guide you, and you could make contact with your spirit guides. Ultimately, an experience of all-embracing unconditional love, a feeling of lightness, or a sense of bliss are signs of great spiritual progress, showing you that your vibration is rising and you are becoming one with Spirit. However, the important thing to remember when meditating is to not have any expectations on what you will experience — to enjoy your meditation time and let your experiences be real and true for you. Like a flowering bud about to open its petals to the sun, so you will blossom in the presence of divine light.

Meditation can be the doorway for higher change, yet Rome was not built in a day, so take each day as it comes as you evolve spiritually through meditation. It is the aim of Supreme Spirit that you do not falter in your ascension, and every time you connect with the light in meditation, you are being heavenly blessed and assisted. Through regular practice of this type of meditation, a gradual augmentation in your vibration will take place until you come to realize the love and joy of Spirit within and without you.

Practice

- Set a suitable time every day to meditate on the light.
- Incorporate meditating with sound.
- Make notes of your experiences.

Step 2
Opening to Your Intuition

Your intuition is an expert at telling you what is for your highest good. It can truthfully inform you of what is going on around you and what another person is like in order to help you make the right choices. For example, your intuition can usually spot whether someone is being honest or not. Of course, there may be other giveaways — like facial expressions, body language, and what is being said — to get an idea about character, and these are to be carefully observed. Yet when you become aware of the accuracy of this divinely tuned-in side, you can instantaneously sense the energy of others and your environment before needing to analyze a situation.

Some of you may have shut down your natural ability to recognize your feelings. To allow the wisdom of them to emerge, you will need to acknowledge the truth about how you are running your life, your feelings about a specific person or a certain situation. For some, this may seem scary, because once you admit your feelings, you might think that you have to change in some way or another. However, not being attentive to your feelings or denying them can slow down your growth.

By being aware of your feelings, you will bring in guidance from your higher self to positively assist you in life. In fact, life's dilemmas can be resolved far more easily and decisions can be made in your best interest and the good of everybody else concerned by taking notice of your feelings. They are there to help you — not just on the odd occasion, but every day, in every circumstance.

You are an intelligent being who knows a lot more than you let yourself admit. In fact, there is nothing that your higher self does not know. Yet when you say to yourself that you do not know about something, you block out the wisdom of your higher self sent to you through your feelings and intuition. However, if you were to tell yourself that you do understand what it is all about or that you know a solution to a current problem, this will aid in calling up the wisdom of your intuition.

The Spiritually Developed Are Intuitive Souls

Genuine spiritual healers can intuitively see or feel positive and negative energy within a person, chakra system, or aura. Some healers may even detect incidents that have happened in a person's life — or even past lives — and can accurately tell you that person's next reincarnation. Enlightened masters also come across as being all-knowing because of their natural affiliation with Spirit, seeing with precision many things about another soul's life path and spiritual development.

Through your own spiritual practices like meditation on the light, your intuition will begin to open and develop, which can result in having telepathic and psychic experiences. These extrasensory qualities are a natural expression of the soul, not abilities that are weird or out of this world. As you reach a higher vibration and consciousness in sync with your soul's light, these abilities will become normal to you.

There are also people who are highly intuitive, who naturally sense the vibrations of others and their surroundings yet are unaware that they are actually picking up on these vibes. This may be you. Take a situation in which you have been happy and relaxed all day until you meet a friend. As you chat, you suddenly start to feel low with a headache coming on. Unless there is any specific medical problem that can account for this feeling, it could be that you have read the current vibration of the other person without actually being aware of what you were doing and then thought that this energy was yours.

Spiritually evolved souls who have not yet recognized their level of spiritual development are usually very sensitive to the energies around them, unaware that they literally pick up on the vibes around them. If this is you, you need to see your sensitivity as a gift, showing you what is and is not love and light around you.

No doubt, you may sometimes feel affected by these more negative and denser energies. Signs of this are feeling drained, irritable, low, or less than your buoyant self after being in someone's home or presence. You could start to be conscious of taking on this person's negative thoughts and feelings, or an image of the person you have recently been with might keep popping into your mind long after being with him or her. In fact, these negative effects can sometimes overwhelm and unbalance you.

Visualization: Clearing Unwanted Energy

- *To help bring you back into balance, place your hands in prayer position at the level of your heart chakra in the middle of your chest.*
- *Look up and out through your third eye.*
- *See a radiant, golden sun shining above you and say to yourself, "Divine light, now harmonize and cleanse my energy."*
- *Light rays are coming down from this sun and enveloping you.*
- *As you feel or observe this light touch your being, begin to see it expand, encompassing the whole of your body — your aura and beyond — until you see yourself in a sphere of white light.*
- *Feel this light bringing a renewed wholeness and balance to your being.*
- *Sense or see this light awaken the light within you.*

If you believe someone's negative energy has affected you, you might want to finish off this energy rebalancing and clearing technique by visualizing the expanding light also enveloping that person. As you do so, let your thoughts be positive and compassionate toward this person.

- *Envisage the person getting better, see the distressed be at peace, or visualize that soul accomplishing good in life.*

If it is a space that has taken you off balance:

- *Imagine that space being filled with this light to help clear it of negative energy.*
- *Lastly, with hands still in prayer position, thank the divine light for assisting you.*

Being Intuitive Means Looking, Listening, and Feeling Inwardly

Your first immediate feelings are usually your most trustworthy and correct. Take a situation where your friend has just introduced you to someone new. Now, some people will go on appearances and even professional status to figure out whether this person is "worthy" or "good." They will instantly accept or deny another by their own or society's standards.

Nonetheless, this shortsighted view may, in the long run, get you into trouble. If on the other hand you listen to your inner world of perception, which literally means you have checked out the vibration of a person or place, it will accurately begin to tell you what you need to know from being in this person's presence. These are not mental judgments but your intuitive soul telling you the underlying personality of this person.

Intuitively reading the energies of others and your surroundings can also guide you in what to say and do next. As you consider what to talk about through the guidance of your intuition, you can generate an air of openness that can have a positive or even healing influence on the people you are with. Balance is all about knowing how to juggle your life in the most effective and harmonious ways. Through your awareness of your feelings and the guidance of your intuition, you will come to understand how to treat each person and circumstance in the most constructive manner.

Example Scenario

You decide to go shopping tomorrow. The next morning arrives, but you feel the energy to shop just is not there and the idea of gardening feels far more attractive. A little voice inside you may even detract you from spending money today. But you take no notice of this inner guidance and force yourself to go to the shopping center because you are going to stick to what you planned. Then on your way to your destination, you find that there are road workers creating a queue of traffic, delaying you from getting to your destination. When you eventually get there, the shop you wanted to go in has unexpectedly closed. It takes trust to follow your instincts.

Go with Your Positive Feelings

Learn to change your mind by sensing when the energy is there or not. Your higher self can go out and look at many probable futures and know what is and is not in your greatest good. This is then sent back to you through your moods and bodily sensations. Do you feel tired or enlivened when thinking about taking a certain path? How does your body feel? Light and positive feelings will suggest the better route for you to take.

Changing your mind from acknowledging your feelings does not mean you are indecisive. It signifies you can see the signpost that will take you on a quicker route to success. In fact, to keep you on your higher path, be ready to change your mind whenever your intuition steers you to.

Your intuition chooses different ways to communicate with you. Higher guidance is always energizing, informing, loving, and illuminating. It will always have your highest good and the highest good of others in mind. It is said that a picture can paint a thousand words, so your soul may well take advantage of that by sending an inner vision to enlighten you. Expanded feelings such as lightness, love, or inner peace are other forms of soul communication, as well as wise and compassionate thoughts to guide you. Seeing an image of light in the space around you when receiving intuitional insights shows you are channeling knowledge, healing, or guidance of great significance from your higher self.

Words are another way to receive a higher guidance from your intuitive self. Although the trouble with words is that you can sometimes misinterpret them or limit the importance of their meaning, which is why your soul will often use more explicit forms of imagery, feeling, and experience to get the message across.

Come out of your rational mind for an experience of the heavenly. In deep meditation, in a state of relaxation, or while just being in the present moment, you may come to experience a greater love or an overwhelming joy — a realization of Supreme Spirit. Such an awakening could be very difficult to put into words for you to understand, but you will never forget a profoundly moving godly experience. Therefore, your feelings are not only there to help guide you on a higher path but also to give you an understanding into the nature of your soul and Supreme Spirit.

Your intuition is divine intelligence. As a beginner recognizing intuition in this manner for the first time, you may think that these experiences are your imagination, something that you consider to be unreal or made up. Yet if imagination did not exist, then it would not be there, so it must have an important function.

Your imagination, in the form of an inner vision, for example, works with your intuitive sight to reveal soul guidance. Many people have very vivid dreams that either come true or signify important messages. Others may see things in or after meditation that bring clarity, healing, or a better understanding to a problem.

Your imagination is one of the greatest gifts you have. It is a powerful tool to develop, as it can help you manifest and realize your life-long dreams, get you in touch with your highest good, and lend a hand at relaying insights. Try spending more time letting your imagination roam to the unlimited heights of what you wish for and you will soon find the statement "it was just my imagination" totally irrelevant!

Your life is like a dream, linked with many other people's dreams that are all being played out at the same time. This all takes place within one great cosmic dream — the dream of Supreme Spirit. When you were born, certain things had been set up to help create your soul's dream in the physical: the people, places, and circumstances. However, since you have been born, you will always have free will to respond to your soul's dream or not. In fact, have you ever felt that you have free will only to a certain point, as if the other half of you feels your life has been already mapped out and that you are, in reality, well on track? To help live out your ideal life, get in contact with your intuition to receive soul guidance and use your imagination to help make your dreams come true.

Everything and everybody is made up of energy, moving at different vibrations. You can check out what is good for you by feeling the vibration of things. Before making any decisions, think about taking a particular path and then see how you feel. A light feeling in your body before embarking on a certain route or while contemplating a certain decision can suggest your highest good.

Experiment with this method in a very practical way to know what is best for you to eat. Place the palm of your dominant hand over different foods or even meals on a menu and sense a feeling of lightness from that palm or a light feeling in the body to indicate beneficial foods for you to eat. Or ask your intuition what would be in your highest good to have for lunch today and then listen inwardly or receive a mental image or taste of that food or dish. Learning how to dowse can help beginners who are not very confident at distinguishing this lighter feeling within.

Practice: How to Dowse

- Write down a list of foods on a piece of paper.
- Take a silver or gold chain and let it hang from your forefinger and thumb. Say, "Light of my soul, what foods are in my highest good to eat?"
- Next, hang the chain over the name of a food and mentally say it. If the chain starts to go back and forth, this usually reveals a negative response. When the chain does not move, this is a sign that this food is neutral — neither good nor bad for you. But if the chain moves around in a circle, it is an indication that this food is favorable for you to eat.

Now, try including these favorable foods in your diet and see how you feel. You can also use dowsing to find out herbal or natural remedies that you may need.

Be attentive to the type of moods you have and how your body feels after eating and drinking certain foods. For example, what do you feel like a few hours after drinking some alcohol, eating meat, or consuming a vegetarian meal? Do you feel depressed, sluggish, or lighter?

Which fabrics allow your chi energy to flow harmoniously? Feel the difference between wearing synthetic materials to that of natural fibers, such as cotton, wool, hemp, or silk. Colors reflect different vibrations and healing qualities too, so follow your intuition when choosing which colors to wear today.

The spiritually accomplished know how to channel divine energy to purify and spiritualize food and drink. They can also reduce harmful side effects of medication and positively change the vibration of where they live and work. Try blessing your meals or environment with spiritual energy. As you hold your hands over your food or out into a room, ask the light to come through you to spiritually bless, harmonize, and energize.

Check to see how you are feeling throughout the day. How do you feel out in nature, playing or cuddling with your children, being with your closest friends, listening to your favorite music, or meditating? Find out and do more of those things that make you feel alive, happy, at peace, loved, and light, for these activities will be in your highest good and can create times when insights or guidance will come through with great clarity.

Thoughts have a powerful energy to them, as what you think, you begin to create! Be more aware of those thoughts that make you feel positive and light and those that have the opposite effect. Remember that every time you use your feelings to perceive the vibration of people, places, and things, you are exercising your intuition like a muscle, and the more you use it and take notice of it, the stronger it will get.

Be awake to the messages that life is showing you. You are living within God's creation. Amid all things, Supreme Spirit is omnipresent. Therefore, the Creator's wisdom and guidance can be seen and heard in the world around you that can jog your memory into greater knowing.

Lyrics to a song may help you remember the power of love. A ten-foot poster billboard could be affirming an important decision that you have just made. You may even over hear words from a conversation of some passersby that uncannily give you a lead to solving a problem.

These outer clairvoyant messages can be found anytime and everywhere, in many different ways and places. They are Spirit conveying love, support, clarity, or a higher direction. You will know when you come across them because somehow they will stand out and catch your eye or attention, accompanied by a sense of rightness that says, "Yes, this is the answer for me."

Meditation: Developing Your Intuition

Remember to go to a quiet place where you will not be disturbed and get yourself in meditation position. If you feel the need, spend a few minutes or so beforehand practicing the breathing technique to calm the mind. It will help center you. Now you are ready to connect with your intuition at will.

- *Breathe normally.*
- *Take your awareness to the area of your third eye chakra, situated between your eyebrows in the middle of your forehead.*
- *With your eyes closed, or half-open, look up and out of this chakra.*
- *The divine light from above touches and awakens this area for you to see and know more clearly.*

For those of you who are beginners at making a stronger connection to your intuition, you might feel this area begin to tingle or pulsate. The loving and wise presence of your higher self is now fully with you.

- *Ask for guidance on any issue for yourself or for another. (In the beginning, only ask about one issue at a time. It might be a decision that you have to make; you may want greater understanding on a problem that you are facing or clarity on a spiritual truth.)*
- *Be receptive to a high and compassionate guidance in the form of feelings, images, or wise and helpful thoughts.*
- *Continue to take as much time as you need to receive these insights.*
- *When you are ready, thank the light and come back into the room, remembering anything that you experienced.*

If you feel you didn't receive anything while meditating, don't think that you are doing anything wrong. You have opened your intuition to a new level. In the day or week ahead, you will be shown what you need to know through new feelings, insights, or even dreams that come up related to the question you asked today.

Further Guidance

- You may want to write down your insights to assist in clarifying your experience or to keep for future reference.
- For some, listening to your intuition in this way for the first time may take a bit of practice. Do not try to force yourself to visualize, hear, or feel anything, as concentrating too hard will defeat the object.
- All requests for guidance are answered, so believe in that. Sometimes you may feel that you did not receive any guidance in meditation, yet later while going about your day or week ahead, you may suddenly get an intuitive insight or a revelation about a requested problem. Once you start listening and accepting your intuitive insights, the more you will become aware of them any time of the day.
- Remember that it is not necessary that you actually see the light at the third eye to know that you are making a connection to Spirit.
- Be aware of how you are feeling throughout your day. Your true essence is light, positive, and cheerful, so learn to change your thoughts and activities to reflect that.
- Lastly, and most importantly, put your positive guidance that you receive from your intuition into action to help bring about your heaven on earth.

Step 3

Master Connection

You may have forgotten that Supreme Spirit is ever-present and that you are, in fact, a part of her/his eternal love and light, yet Spirit never fails to wake those of you who really care to remember her/him and the truth of your divinity. To assist you in recalling and becoming more of your intrinsic nature, the saints and enlightened ones come to guide those who are ready to self-realize. Like shepherds to a flock of gone-astray sheep, they appear to lend a hand in directing those lost souls back home to truth.

The Presence of an Enlightened One Is an Act of Love

These leaders of light may be living now or may have been a part of this or another world in some distant past. Nonetheless, whether they are presently alive or not, these educators of a higher wisdom are forever accessible to help lift your vibration and direct you toward more evolved ways of living and self-realization.

A lucky few may already be in physical contact with such a spiritual master. However, for the majority of us, they reside ethereally present, and for that reason, your special master or group of angels who are working with you in this lifetime may go completely unrecognized by you. Yet to help you in your ascension, it can be beneficial to know exactly who your particular bringers of light are.

An individual master or your group of enlightened messengers may have already made an appearance to you at some time in your life. You might have been in much anguish and prayed for help, only to find yourself unexpectedly taken back by the inner sight of such a great one. Perhaps an enlightened being showed itself to you in meditation, you may have dreamed or daydreamed of meeting one of your guides, or you might have been given a picture of a saint in a time of much need.

Being in the presence or intuitively in touch with such a hallowed teacher can make you feel like you are in the company of a living god. Through their illumination, spiritual masters can demonstrate an awakening of Spirit within you, and as your vibration rises, you may perceive these transmitters of peace and love with you or around others.

For some of you who are more spiritually evolved, you may be able to telepathically communicate with the masters of light, receiving the word of Spirit and loving supervision to inspire and help you and others grow. Some spiritual healers may also sometimes see such avatars clairvoyantly, especially while giving healing treatments or counseling. Seeing such visions usually indicates that, consciously or unconsciously, spiritual help has been taken on by the one receiving spiritual healing or counseling and that there will be a positive transformation or a restoration of health for that person concerned.

However, do be cautious. Most healers keep such impressions to themselves unless they feel that it is of real benefit to the person being healed. Be aware of those wolves in sheep's clothing who are only interested in making a lot of money out of other people's suffering or spiritual growth and who want to feed their overinflated egos with false practices. If a so-called spiritual healer or teacher makes you feel uncomfortable in any way, puts imaginary fears into your head, or leaves you with a substantial dent in your pocket for little help, maybe you should seriously think about whether to return.

Nonetheless, do not be put off, because there are some genuine bringers of the light out there who ask for reasonable payments for their work. If you feel empowered, positively helped, honored, and truly wiser after being with such a person, then you will have some indication that your guide is here to truly help and is worth his or her weight in gold.

So where may you find your special ones? Unless you are living at the foot of the Himalayas or are auspicious enough to trace one living nearby, you might think that the materialization of one so mystic as this is rather rare and elusive. But you need not become disheartened. Through divine service and their omnipresent spirit, they come forth to whoever calls on them, radiating love, understanding, and guidance, whether they have already departed from physical life or are living now on the other side of the planet. Your designated spiritual comrades are immediately yours at your intention and hope for them to be with you. To make a master connection, all you need is to be ready and willing to receive them.

You Will Begin to Create What You Concentrate On

Next is a simple yet effective way to make a connection to any enlightened spiritual teacher. By meditating on the figure or picture of any enlightened being, you can facilitate your vibration to rise to where a feeling of peace, joy, or wisdom can be found.

Take a picture or photograph of any spiritual teacher of your choice. Shiva, Paramahansa Yogananda, Buddha, Jesus Christ, Jiddu Krishnamurti, the Virgin Mary, Lord Krishna, John the Baptist, Saint Francis of Assisi, Gandhi, the Dalai Lama, and Babaji are just a few of the very many well-known teachers who have and are still helping to bring the message of Supreme Spirit to assist you in remembering who you are. Perhaps you know of a less-famous divine being or saint you would like to connect with — like a Native American chief — or some of you may feel more attracted to drawings or figures of the archangels or the disciples of one of these holy men or women. To find your specific leaders of light, browse the Internet or go to your local library, bookstore, spiritual center, church, or religious temple. Find drawings and photographs of saints, angels, bodhisattvas, spiritual teachers, deities, disciples, and gurus, choosing the ones that you feel most attracted to and that you seem to have a real affinity with. Now you are ready to connect with any one of your chosen masters more profoundly.

Master Gazing

- *Make sure that you are sitting alone where it is quiet and where you will be undisturbed.*
- *Take a picture, photograph, or figure of an enlightened being that you would like to make a more profound connection with.*
- *Begin by concentrating on the face of this special being; look directly into his or her eyes. The eyes, known as the windows to the soul, are where you will make a powerful soul-to-soul connection.*

- *Take your time to just restfully look at the image of this liberated being. See the beauty in him or her, taking your time to note how you feel as you do so. Is there any specific soul virtue, such as inner peace, compassion, or great wisdom that this spiritual master seems to emit more of?*

It is here that some of you more-evolved souls may begin to hear your inner voices speak clearly on a higher wisdom or guidance. For those who are beginners to this type of telepathic meditation, it may seem like you are talking to yourself or making it all up. However, such highly intelligent and wise direction from any enlightened one will be compassionate, wise, positively helpful, and healing for you and to all those concerned. This should be considered a blessing.

- *Continue to meditate on the figure of this revered one for as long as you can, as this will assist you in lifting your vibration.*
- *When you feel you have finished, thank this master from your heart.*
- *Reflect on any good feelings or positive guidance you were given.*

Further Guidance

It is important to go with whatever you experience in this meditation. Some of you may begin to see light around your chosen spiritual master while some may feel your hearts touched with love and peace. If you do begin to see anything unusual — like marks, dark spots, or patches on this master's body or face — while concentrating on the figure, this quite magnificently signifies that this master is awakening you to your own energetic blockages by mirroring them to you.

Example Scenario

Joanna had trouble trusting in her intuition and felt quite lost and uncertain of decisions because of her disbelief in her inner voice and gut feelings. As she carried out the master gazing meditation, she started to see a dark patch at the third eye of the saint that she was concentrating on. The third eye is the center of the sixth sense and higher perception, and she was being shown that energetically this chakra was closed through her lack of belief in her intuition. Through this saint mirroring her problem to her in this way, she proceeded to have some Reiki healing on this chakra and flower essence therapy to get her brow chakra functioning harmoniously. She soon began to listen to and trust in her inner voice and intuitive sight again.

If you like, make your own special collection of pictures of the saints you feel are helping you raise your consciousness and vibration. Then practice the master gazing meditation wherever you like at home. In the area of where you meditate, perhaps you could place pictures or photos of your chosen guides or masters to receive their ever-present love, higher direction, and light.

The Masters Are Channels of Unconditional Love

Some of the timeless masters will resonate more with you than others. You will know who your given spiritual teachers are because you will feel a kind of recognition that their presence has always been with you, guiding and protecting you ever since you were born, as if somehow you are in their hearts and they are in yours. An affiliation of deep love and renewed friendship can be found by making a more conscious connection to your specific saints; some of you can weep with joy at seeing a picture of them for the first time. This reaction most definitely concludes that this master is one of your guides.

To rediscover your guides brings about an air of companionship, inner peace, comfort, unconditional love, and joy. For some of you, it can feel like you are going back to your spiritual home to be reunited with your devoted family of angels. If you have found it difficult to rely on others for support and help before, it can be a great relief to recognize and communicate with your ever-dependable guide or team of light.

Such a holy encounter can encourage a soul awakening within you, even if your spiritual path has lain somewhat dormant up till now. Creating a link to Spirit through any liberated being can give you the necessary insights, strength, and circumstances — which you might call miracles — to lend a hand in resolving your current struggles and direct you to your highest good. Just one look at a heavenly messenger can bring about many blessings, initiating a more conscious relationship with this master or group of guides.

You can unite with the heavenly wherever and whoever you are. Whether you are sitting in the sacredness of a church or temple or sitting in your own home, light, love, and higher wisdom can be yours through master gazing. The masters' work is for those who are choosing to grow spiritually, sending out devoted assistance, spiritual knowledge, and healing to all those who are open to receive it.

It is the love of Supreme Spirit, the compassion of these spiritual masters, and the level of your spiritual development that give you this good fortune to help realize Spirit in this way. Nevertheless, making a connection to one of them does not mean that you have to take up or be associated with any form of related religion — Christian, Buddhist, Hindu, or others — unless, of course, you have a true desire to do so.

You Will Come to Know Your True Nature by Experiencing Spirit

The work of spiritual masters is to assist you in awakening to your own light. They appear to empower you, not to take it away, and although they spend the majority of their lives trying to tell us the truth, they do not always do so. They like to point the way for you to experience and find out what your truth is.

Instead of letting others tell you who you are and what does and does not work for you, continue to meditate on the light at your third eye (see the focus of light meditation in step 1) to find your truth. Look around you and observe the world today to know what brings you joy and empowers you, others, and the planet. Try out a new thought or activity to see if it benefits you, for you will need to discover your own way and believe in yourself if you are to become your own master.

Christ Consciousness Is Inherent in All Creation

God consciousness can be found in every atom of the universe. It is not only outside of you but within you, present in all creation. Each of us has been given the potential to realize and come from this higher level of being. Still, it is not a question of whether you are capable of being your soul's light and love on Earth; it is a matter of choice. The second coming of Christ means spiritual transformation. Not that the savior will be reborn and save you some day, but that there will be a second coming of Christ within you — a spiritual awakening and remembering.

As the true advocates of the Absolute hold a focus of light and love for those choosing to become more of their full potential, they are always ready to give assistance when asked. Making an association with any fully realized master can give you a higher understanding of life that, if you take notes of your experiences and insights, can reveal a timeless significance and spiritual weight read many years after acquiring them.

The Grand Master of All runs through all the illuminated masters, through all souls, and through all of life. In the course of a more conscious relation to these shining stars of peace, you can come to remember more about who you really are and the unconditional love and joy of your soul and Supreme Spirit in the light of day.

Visualization: Meeting Your Spiritual Master

The location in this visualization is set in the heart of some sacred mountains. However, if you so wish, feel free to choose your own setting by letting your imagination take you to an appropriate place that will help you connect with one of your masters of light.

- *Prepare yourself for this visualization by either sitting up in a comfortable chair or by lying down.*
- *Close your eyes and look up and out of your third eye, connecting with the light.*
- *As you breathe in, imagine that you are breathing this light into your being.*
- *As you breathe out, feel yourself begin to relax deeply, allowing any bodily tension and thoughts about your day to disappear.*
- *Breathe this way a few times until you feel yourself become calm and peaceful.*
- *Breathe normally now.*

Suddenly, you find yourself standing in nature. As you look around, you admire the scene of a splendid mountain range. Above the peaks sits a chalky-white new moon and a magnificent double rainbow. Reflecting on the beauty here, you see a path leading up to the slopes beyond.

- *Take that path now.*

As you begin your journey upward, you immediately begin to feel light and energized by this magical place. Some of you might feel so light that you begin to see yourself rapidly moving or even flying to your destination.

- *Continue your journey, appreciating the nature around you as you move on.*

Before you know it, you arrive at a high plateau. This is your destination. As you look how far you have come, you admire the breathtaking sight of an array of glistening, snow-capped mountain peaks against a pink and orange sunset.

As you glance over to a nearby tree, you notice the figure of a person standing by it. You have not seen this person before, yet the face seems strangely familiar to you. Immediately, you are taken in with this person's loving smile and gentle eyes.

- *Go over to greet this person.*

How do you feel in the person's presence? Is he or she living now or from the past? Perhaps you know the person's name? Do you recognize this person?

This gracious being is your spiritual master, or guide. Also know that you might have other connections to other spiritual teachers who are helping you in this lifetime as well.

You sit down and face each other. Without saying anything, you immediately feel a spiritual and loving connection to this master.

- *Feel a vibration of love touch your heart.*

Your master has a special message for you. You receive this message in the form of words, images, or feelings. This great one stands up and places a hand on your crown, brow, or heart chakra to assist you in making a stronger connection to Spirit.

- *Take your time here to experience this.*
- *When you are ready, graciously give thanks to this master for blessing you today.*
- *Know that this enlightened one will always be available to you for spiritual wisdom, guidance, and love.*
- *Open your eyes and come back into the room, taking your time to reflect on this wonderful meeting.*

Further Guidance

Use this visualization to find out about other enlightened ones and guides who are working with you in this lifetime.

Step 4
Being Happy

Happiness is a soul virtue, an expression of your true self. On your path of ascension, it is essential that you cultivate a joyful attitude to assist in letting the light of your soul shine through. Nonetheless, happiness, at many times, can possibly elude you. You may think your happiness will come from having material things, such as buying a better car, getting a bigger house, or finding a new partner, and it can be true that you get an initial buzz when first having something new. However, the novelty soon wears off and the feeling of newfound contentment begins to fade, leaving you searching for something else that will produce a hint of pleasure.

Problems can also arise in your life. Will the materialistic things that you then own have a solution to your dilemma? The secret to longer-lasting happiness must therefore come from within, and by changing your thoughts, actions, and attitudes about life can lend a hand in achieving this natural state whenever you wish.

Smile

When you find yourself concentrating on troubling thoughts, try smiling. It can take you out of a negative inner space, reduce stress, and lift your spirits. Try smiling and then think of a negative thought — it is quite difficult to do.

Smiling when you meet someone declares that you have good self-esteem, that you accept the other person, and it reveals openness on your part to be accepted. A smile can also help put another at ease, especially when that someone is upset. A smile will encourage the other person to be more of his or her cheerful self. So a simple smile can be considered not only as an expression of cheerfulness but as a look of love.

However, there are some who prefer to show a miserable face even when there seems to be no apparent understandable reason. Those who always seem negative do not usually want a happier life. They have either fallen into the depressing pattern of being glum or, believe it or not, they actually like wallowing in dejectedness. They see it as effective in getting others to feel sorry for them or in attracting negative attention.

Sadly, these types see their blue states as being far more important than the lighthearted moods of those around them and will hold on to their misery at all costs. If you are associating with such people, make sure that your optimistic and merry attitude is much stronger than their gloom and doom; otherwise, you could eventually be affected by their miserable disposition.

The vibration in a room can be raised through just one relaxed, heartfelt smile. Just look at the pure joy you get from seeing a baby smile. It can make everyone feel good. Still, you can always tell whether people smiling to cover up something or they are being false. So to feel the real benefits of smiling, smile sincerely from the heart.

Be Lighthearted

Being dedicated to your spiritual path is all very worthy, but it is essential that it does not become dry without fun and a sense of humor. Experiencing Supreme Spirit is the ultimate joy, and by being cheery and bright, you will be expressing your divinity.

Still fresh from the pureness of Spirit, children remember to express the playfulness that adults tend to forget because of the seriousness of it all. Evolved souls can express their lighthearted side by laughing at themselves and seeing the funny side of things, especially when events do not go the way they plan. A sense of humor can put things into perspective and take the tension out of life.

Be Thankful

Those who count their blessings tend to be more satisfied in life. Being grateful for the good that you have now and not taking it all for granted helps the mind concentrate on the positive, and that will lead you to become happier, more optimistic, and literally lighter.

Getting bogged down by the negative can cloud the infinite good that life has to offer. Although most of us have probably experienced difficult times in our lives, if you can see the good that results from a troubling period, you will probably realize that you are now a lot wiser for that experience or that it changed you positively in some way. Whatever the circumstances, there will always be a silver lining to your nimbus.

After coming through a difficult phase and seeing the light, you may feel a deep sense of gratitude to Supreme Spirit for showing you the way forward and helping you realize something significant about yourself or how life works. However, gratitude should not only be expressed when you have come out of trouble, transformed for the better, or even when your prayers have been answered. Being grateful for the nice things you have or that happened today can benefit your sense of contentment and help lift your vibration.

There is nothing more effective to help you receive more of the unlimited plenty of Supreme Spirit than being grateful. There are so many things you can give thanks for — a home to live in, a warm bed to sleep in, or even the food you have in the fridge are just some of the everyday things that we can all take for granted.

Perhaps you are healthy or someone was kind to you today. Every day try giving thanks for the good that happened to you and for the good things you have already. Saying your thank-yous out loud or by writing them down will amplify the power of gratitude for even more abundance to come into your life and open your heart to receive more. Ultimately, giving thanks to Supreme Spirit not only attracts more plenty into your life; it can also calm and balance your emotions, supporting you to feel happy.

When you appreciate the beauty of the world, you engage in the miracle of life. An evening's coral sunset, the perfection of every laid-out petal to form the loveliness of a flower, the uplifting effect of your favorite music — all are proof that life is positively working with you. In these appreciative moments, life is actually speaking back to you, assuring you that you are doing well, that you are on your right path, and that everything now is just perfect for you to grow. Being aware and grateful of the simple marvels of the world around you will help you relax and put a smile on your face.

Let Go and Bring in the New

In order for more happiness to flow into your life, sometimes you have to pinpoint what is making you feel the opposite: unhappy. Many of you might know what is making you feel less than satisfied — for example, an unfulfilling relationship or a difficult and unrewarding job. For the rest of you, it could be something that you cannot quite put your finger on, like an unhelpful belief or a pattern that you are unaware that you hold or do.

Sometimes we find it hard to let go, even when something is making our lives stressful or miserable. The idea that something better will not come to replace the thing that you would like to let go of often stops you from getting rid of the joyless and painful. Yet only by letting go of those things that no longer serve you do you make space for new things to come in. As you evolve, learn to change those things in your life that no longer reflect the new vibration that you are becoming. Know that if you feel it is time to let go of something that no longer brings you joy, there will be something better to take its place.

Supreme Spirit helps those who help themselves, so make the effort to do everything you can to turn an unwanted situation around. Many people will go on for years putting up with the same old unhappy circumstances or relationships, doing nothing to change it, which can lead to stagnation and resentment.

Look and you will find for there is a solution to every problem. To discover the root of your concerns it may be well worth your while searching for the spiritual cause. This may mean looking into new and alternative ways to bring about release and healing. Read new books on spiritual development, maybe choose some type of holistic healing to help turn your health problems around, or get some spiritual counseling or divine healing. In the depths of meditation while looking out of your third eye, ask for help on any issue you would like to improve. Then receive feedback from your intuition or wait and see what unexpectedly comes your way in the days ahead.

Feeling guilty about moving on can also hinder you from embracing the new. Always go for what brings you happiness. Put plainly and simply, anything that you get joy from doing will be in your highest good and will be in the highest good for others, even if it initially does not seem like it to the other person. In fact, guilt has no real beneficial effects, serving only to make you or another feel bad, so try to refrain from holding on to guilt or projecting it onto others.

Not being able to let go of the past can also make you feel sad. Some of you may well have had traumatic or troubling times in your childhood or as a young adult that you hold deep within, which stops you from being happy or secure now. Realizing and accepting what you felt in those past circumstances is the key to letting it all go. This is a time when you may need to bring to the surface your hidden sorrows or hurts of the past. Talking over what happened with someone you trust and truly wants to listen can help, or you may like to be alone and chat inwardly to your higher self or God about it. Others may look to the past with regrets, perhaps looking toward your unfulfilled dreams that never came true. Still, you will be making the process of bringing in the new even more difficult if you continue to constantly reflect on past regrets and unhappy events.

Constantly dwelling on unhappy times in your day will only bring past negative energy into the present to make you feel less than happy today. And that can even attract more unhappy events into your present life, because whatever you put your mind on, you will begin to create. Having compassion and understanding the problems and issues a person was facing at the time when he or she upset you can assist you in releasing your past (help with forgiveness is given in step 5). If the unhappy past is constantly on your mind, then find the feeling that you feel about it all — not so much what happened — and you will be on your way to release and inner peace again. Do not let your mind take you over, because the mind loves to concentrate on negativity. Now is the time to forget your unhappiness of former years and concentrate on what you now want to create. Then act on that and do not look back.

In every moment, you have the chance to create your life anew. Break free from old unhelpful patterns by considering newness in everything you see and do. Viewing everything as new, as if you are seeing or experiencing it for the first time just like a child, will help you create a more wonderful life. Finding wonder and awe in nature and things you just take for granted will make you feel in high spirits and lift your vibration. You will realize that your unlimited joy is in your hands because of how you choose to feel and be in every fresh moment.

Set Your Expectations Free

When things do not meet our expectations, we can become disappointed and thus discontented. Dream about what you want to create next through the image of who you want to be and what you want to feel. Envision scenes of successful future happenings related to your desire, and then take action to bring it forth through the guidance of your intuition. Then release any expectation of how this longing will finally take shape.

Example Scenario

Helen, a nineteen-year-old who just passed her A-levels with good grades, then had to decide what profession she would like to be in. She was brought up on a farm and loved helping out and taking care of the many different animals there. Helen decided she wanted to continue to work with animals and would like to be a vet.

She studied for years on a veterinary course, only to find that once she had passed her final exam, it all felt a bit anticlimactic, as being a general vet was not something that she now wanted to carry on pursuing. She realized that her true passion was to specialize in equine (horse) veterinary medicine, and with her new interest in acupuncture and herbs, she now felt she only wanted to work with horses incorporating alternative therapies to help treat them.

Remember, the process of getting to your destination is far more important than the outcome. It will be your experience of that learning journey and who you realize you are in that period that really counts, not just the final result. In addition, life may have something better suited to you than your current expectations.

Meditation: Exploring Your Happiness

- *Lie down on the floor.*
- *Let your arms and legs relax.*
- *Let your jaw relax.*
- *Take some deep breaths: As you breathe in, imagine that you are breathing in joy. As you breathe out, see your present-day thoughts and concerns being released.*
- *Feel yourself becoming lighter and lighter.*

- *Sense yourself feeling happy and at peace.*
- *Breathe normally now.*
- *Look up and out through your third eye chakra.*
- *See or imagine a bright sun from this area.*
- *Let the radiance of this sun touch your whole being.*
- *Ask what you can think, say, or do to bring more happiness into your life.*
- *Receive this guidance through images, feelings, or a message.*
- *Imagine yourself being this new way that your intuition is now showing you.*

How do feel as you imagine yourself being this way? What expression do you have on your face? Can you see how this new way of being benefits your happiness and perhaps the happiness of others too?

- *Ask if there is anything else that you could let go of to help you become a happier person.*
- *Take your time to receive this insight.*
- *When you are ready, sincerely thank the light, and commit to putting this higher guidance into action.*

Further Guidance

If you do not initially get any insights in this meditation, do not worry. You will most likely come to realize something about how to increase your happiness in the time after or in the days following this meditation.

You can use this meditation to help you feel and express other soul virtues. Ask the light how you can bring in more peace, self-love, creativity, or any other soul quality that you might want to increase in your life.

Choose to Think in Positive Ways

Positive and happy thoughts have a high vibration that will lift your energy and attract good in your life. In comparison, negative beliefs contribute to dragging your energy down, and that not only makes you feel low but can have a detrimental effect on the way your body and mind function too. Understanding that your true self is inherently positive, loving, joyful, and good can give you the strength to reform any of those less-than-positive thoughts about yourself that you may have.

Training yourself to be more of your true and happy self means being aware of how you think, speak, and act. Limiting, fearful, or negative beliefs that you hold are like little demons that want to put you down and take your joy or another's away. Speak no evil, hear no evil, and say no evil — this will support you in keeping your energy lighter.

Look at Where You Are Coming From

Start by being conscious of what you are thinking and how you are being while doing the mundane: cooking dinner, getting ready in the morning, or going to work.

Example Scenario

A busy mother who comes home from work in the evenings has a lot to do. In the back of her mind, she worries that if she does not get her child into bed at a certain time every night, her youngster will wake up tired and therefore not able to concentrate well at school. At night she hurries around with this anxiety in mind, trying to get everything done, which eventually makes her short tempered and impatient.

Of course, nighttime may be busy, and the child probably does need to be asleep at a reasonable hour, but wouldn't it be better to prioritize what is more important? Wouldn't an environment of peace and happiness be far more beneficial to the mother's overall well-being and for all those concerned around her? Could her child go to bed half an hour later? She could delegate some of the work she has to do in the evenings, or maybe change her routine to create a more relaxed and pleasing atmosphere rather than her child going to sleep on time with a stressed and grumpy parent.

Be aware of those everyday and less-apparent fearful thoughts and scenarios that can take you off course from being content and stress-free. Make happiness come first on your list of priorities, altering both your mind and routine to support you in being stress-free. It is not what you do but how you do things that is important.

In our day and age, we are seen as hard working and efficient for continually doing things. From a higher perspective, though, life is in fact all about *being*, not doing — being that loving, jovial, compassionate, serene, creative, wise, calm, positive, generous (to name but a few descriptors) true self and then doing things that reflect your light.

Being any soul quality can benefit your inner contentment. Take the feeling of inner peace — being peaceful is dynamic! Your body, mind, and emotions all react well to this state, which can help you to make higher decisions and assist you in getting things done more efficiently than constantly rushing around. In fact, hurrying to complete something can make you feel harassed and short tempered, and it does not necessarily get you anywhere faster.

Pacify Your Fears

Worrying about the future can make you afraid and stressed. Take note: If you are projecting enough fearful thoughts about anything, you will begin to attract those things that you are actually scared of. To soothe your emotions and initiate a more agreeable tomorrow, try thinking of a winning upshot rather than a hopeless or fruitless one.

If you happen to be going through a difficult time and are feeling fearful about your future, remember that this uneasy period cannot go on forever. There is a natural cycle, a beginning and end to everything. Understand that some of our most trying times are there to help propel us to live in new and higher ways. In these unsettling periods, take time to be still, be quiet, and go within. Call on your angels and guides for comfort and support. Have faith in Supreme Spirit to assist you in turning your life around for the better, and keep listening to your intuition for guidance.

Life Exists to Bring About Our Highest Good

Nevertheless, there are times when something can happen to unstabilize us. Maybe you have been unexpectedly made redundant or your partner decides he or she wants to break off your relationship. If you are already feeling upset, the best thing is to admit your feelings. Yet as soon as you can, let go and move on as quickly as you can. Resist making yourself a permanent victim of the situation, for there will be something important here for you to realize.

There are no coincidences in this world. You may be feeling disappointed, yet if you were really honest with yourself, perhaps you had a deep urge to change your career, or maybe you did not have much time to see your partner. Faced with what you may consider to be unfortunate, know that life will have your best interests at heart, even if you cannot see that now. This will end your low self-esteem. Maybe your present adversity is testing you to follow your dreams, find your talents, or change your life direction. Or maybe life is making you wake up to how you have been. Once you find the reason for your dilemma, you can move on with gladness, not sadness. For clarity in understanding a difficult situation and help in turning it around, practice the "opening to your intuition" meditation in step 2.

Be How You Want to Feel

Do not wait for something to happen for you to feel happy. Be happy now! Many of us feel that we need so much to be happy. Nonetheless, if you choose to be cheerful in the present moment, without any condition, and you discipline yourself to be this positive, after a few days or so you will start to feel a whole lot better about your life. Not only will your health improve as your bodily cells react harmoniously to thoughts and acts of a higher vibration like happiness, but you will soon find yourself attracting people and opportunities that reflect your buoyant outlook to support you in living a more satisfied life.

Give Joyfully

Giving assists those who are in need of help and can make the giver feel glad for being generous or helpful. The best thing about having an ever-sufficient supply is that we can readily share it with others. Think of all those people who have contributed to making you feel special by freely giving their time, help, love, or money.

Through the act of giving, you are literally saying that there is always enough, which helps an ever-flowing abundance to keep coming through you to support you and others in being more content. However, how you give is as important as the gift itself. Give with a feeling of joy in your heart, not through a sense of obligation. A small present given with warmth and pleasure feels far nicer to the receiver and to the giver than some substantial gift given dutifully.

Learn to give without expecting anything back from the person who you give to. Do not be disappointed if you invite a couple over to dinner but they never reciprocate the invitation. What you give out, you will get back. Some day in the future, some other friend will come your way and receive you hospitably.

Some of us more caring souls are big givers in time, advice, and resources, yet there may be somebody who, despite our readily being benevolent, does not appreciate the worth of our favors. Any person who does not value your lovely ways will not be receiving the love that you are giving out, which can be disheartening to you. Offer to those who partake with gratitude and will truly gain from your plenty or kindness.

Be Kind

Kind people tend to be happier people. Caring and kind people naturally think well of others and their actions naturally demonstrate a kind heart. Being nice, generous, and compassionate usually comes naturally to the spiritually minded and thus brings them and others considerable joy.

Make friends. The support and care we get from our family, friends, and neighbors contributes greatly to our inner happiness. In a caring community, you will encounter happier individuals, yet those who only concern themselves with having more material wealth, who do their best to compete and show off what they have, only bring dissatisfaction, greed, and envy to the neighborhood. Such lesser ways only serve to separate us, causing loneliness and jealousy within society.

In this day and age, there are too many people concerned with what they can get from others and having their own selfish needs met. However, such ways do not bring about true inner contentment. The kind-hearted are always looked after because they demonstrate that there is always enough love, money, and resources available.

Is there anyone you could give to, say kind words to, or do something nice for who would benefit from your charitable ways to create a sense of happiness in you both? See yourself doing thoughtful acts like holding a door open for someone, telling friends how much you appreciate them, or giving someone the bigger slice of cake. See that what you give out from a loving heart will come back to you doubled. However, if you are being kind and giving to those around you but are not seeing that thoughtfulness come back, maybe you need to learn to receive more and be kinder to yourself. Perhaps you feel you do not deserve to be loved and befriended.

Be Open to Receive

Receiving can make you content too. Our true selves feel and are naturally abundant. What, then, can stop us from receiving a plentiful, happy life and accomplishing our dreams? Limiting ideas to what we can have and deserve and a lack of self-worth. Who taught us those beliefs? Such thoughts close our hearts and deny us the ever-bounteous good available. Spirit may be open-handed to bestow gifts of happiness or prosperity, but your lack of self-worth or self-belief may keep saying that you are not good enough or even that there is not enough.

Every time you say that there is an insufficient supply of anything, that something positive cannot happen to you, or that your dreams cannot come true, you are denying the love of Supreme Spirit to help you create a happy life. Your will is Supreme Spirit's will, and she/he is the provider of all things. Spirit's benevolent unconditional love can work through many different sources to bring you your delight if your thoughts are open and supportive to the idea of such unlimited goodwill.

Learn to receive what you are given. Something or some person may come into your life but, because it does not meet up with your expectations, you may think that you are not getting what you wanted and thus feel disappointed. Nonetheless, your higher self will always give you what is in your highest good, and by knowing that, you will be more willing to accept what comes your way with joy.

Recognize Your Soul Mates

It is fundamental that you spend time with people who love you, support you, and bring you joy. Avoid putting yourself in the presence of others who do not honor you or think highly of you.

To know your soul buddies, look past the physical appearance and feel that of the soul. In today's society we can be indoctrinated to think that we must find the perfect Barbie or Ken as an ideal mate or someone with financial status to be our best pal. If you rely on appearances and status, you can easily look past those who are here to be your loving friends or spiritual comrades.

These special relationships encourage you to grow and will help you know your purpose in life. Your soul mates will be there when situations get tough and to share your joy in more fortunate times. Being with your special companions is an uplifting experience as ease, joy, and unconditional love are generated just by being together. These particular relationships empower both parties because each of you sees the other's greatness and potential. This is, in fact, the purpose of all relationships: to always see who the other person truly is, a unique and special being, and be capable of encouraging that.

Recognize who your soul mates are. They may be people in your family, a friend, a teacher, or even a guru who you feel you had other lifetimes with. Seek out your special angels by following your instincts when meeting new people and feeling an uncommon pleasure and ease when you're together.

Nevertheless, be aware that the negative and less-liked people in your life can, in their own way, show you something important about yourself. You don't have to spend substantial time with these types, but maybe a person who is not very nice to you at work is actually helping you move to a better job or making you address your lack of self-respect. Everyone you come into contact with can help you be more of your higher self.

Make Love

Anything that brings you true joy can be considered holy. Sex, for example, is Supreme Spirit's wonderful gift to celebrate a loving relationship and liberate the soul, and it can even create life. However, there are still some who think that those on a spiritual path should refrain from having sex.

Sex can not only be a very amorous and pleasurable experience but sexual energy used in its highest form can be moved up from your base chakra (at the bottom of your spine) to your crown chakra (at the top of your head) to raise your consciousness. This is known as tantric sex, and sex used in this way can be healing and enlightening. Therefore, the sacred act of making love can be put aside by the spiritually developed or not, knowing that it will not make you less spiritual if you decide to partake in it.

A healthy sex life is one in which there is mutual consent to having sex together in which two individuals are in a committed relationship and want to show their affection and attraction to each other through sex. As you make love, begin by exchanging some loving and appreciative words to each other to help open your hearts. Imagine that all your seven chakras are working in harmony with your partner's. While feeling any sensations in your body, including orgasms, hold off your climax and literally breathe this nice feeling all the way up your spine to the top of your head at your crown chakra. Hold your breath and this energy there for as long as you can. Then just see where you go and what spiritual awakenings you can tap into.

Let sex be fun, fresh, loving, lighthearted, romantic, and even outrageous if you want, preferably taking your time about it too! For those of you who want to know more about how to get in touch with a higher consciousness through sex, there are many books and courses available on tantric sex.

Life Was Created to Be an Enjoyable Experience

Remember to get the most out of your day by making your life more interesting, enjoyable, and fun. We can get so wrapped up in trying to reach our goals and destinations that we can sometimes overlook the importance of actually getting pleasure from each day. One lifetime can seem like the length of a second — relatively short — compared to the life of the universe. Before you know it, you may find that you have been so serious in striving for certain accomplishments, including enlightenment, that you actually forget to enjoy the process.

Take the time to nurture yourself. Listen to your favorite music, go for a walk in the countryside, or make your favorite dish. No two days in your life will be the same, so whatever you are doing, try to make what seems ordinary fresh and new. Life is never boring, so do not try to make it so.

Find your purpose in life by doing what makes you happy and enlivens you, what makes you feel you are becoming the person you want to be. Your heartfelt dreams help to show you what you are here on Earth to do. What inspires and enlivens you? It could be growing a small vegetable garden, running a large company, developing your spiritual side, or all three! If at present you cannot do what most motivates you full-time, make a commitment to do this activity when you can — even if it is just once a week — for a sense of fulfillment. Once you start, you will find yourself making more time to do this much-loved activity. In step 7 you will realize more about your special purpose.

Why spend your life doing something that you do not enjoy? If some activity does not benefit you, then it will not assist anyone else, either. Anything that you really love doing and that makes you feel joyful will be in your highest good to do and thus will positively affect others.

Learn to Be Detached

Being detached does not mean being cold, unsympathetic, or uncompassionate toward another; it means letting that person go his or her own way. Firstly, all people have free will to do and create the life that they choose, and nobody has the right to interfere with that and what makes them happy. Secondly, to understand why a person acts or reacts in a certain way, you would have to be a mind reader because what a person thinks, that person will create.

For instance, if someone always reacts suspiciously to the goodwill of others, you might conclude that this person has a belief not to trust in the generosity of others and therefore closes his or her heart to kindness and friendship. By understanding where people are coming from (in their minds), you can be far more forgiving and detached about the transgressions of others, and such people will have less effect on you feeling good.

However, if you are already feeling hurt or let down by someone, perhaps your best bet is to talk over this issue with those concerned. Tell them how you feel in an assertive and calm way that respects you both. You will feel a whole lot happier about a niggling situation once you express your feelings and know the reason for their reaction. Once you have both expressed how you feel, if possible, end the discussion by finding the middle ground where you can somehow resolve your differences and feel happier about the situation. Talking in this way can bring light to an upsetting situation and bring about inner peace on both sides.

Some of you more gentle and loving souls can feel hurt by the actions and words of those around you, especially when it comes to those close to you. Learn to be strong and unmoved in your happiness. Others may not understand you, your talents, or your dreams, but you do. Perhaps those people concerned feel jealous or inferior to you. Loving yourself means believing in and respecting yourself, and if necessary, being assertive and standing up for yourself. Be clear on what you will and will not stand for. Some of you would feel a lot happier if you supported yourselves in this way. As you come to love and accept who you are, you will find yourself being more detached to the less encouraging around you.

Get Things in Perspective

Are you aware of what takes away your sense of joy? If something is bothering you that seems life-threatening, appears damaging to your health and well-being or that of another, or creates an unharmonious or unhealthy environment, then you may want to speak out and act.

Or is it that you have to have those less important things a certain way? Many people make a huge fuss and get themselves really upset over things that are relatively trivial. Train yourself not to get bogged down with the petty and unimportant. Instead, concentrate on making your life and work joyful.

Be Happy Now

Your happiness is not in the past or some distant future. When you commit to being happy now, troubles from the past will seem meaningless and you will create more happiness for your future.

As your vibration rises through growing spiritually and meditating on the light regularly, the omnipresence of Supreme Spirit will one day become apparent to you — an incomparable, wondrous joy that seems to smile through everything and everywhere. By experiencing the ultimate joy, you will come to realize that you are this joy too.

Visualization: Awakening to Your Higher Nature

Concentrating on the figure of any enlightened being will help you raise your vibration and awaken spiritually. Here, you will be visualizing the divine being of contentment and spiritual liberation — Buddha. Buddha teaches us that our attainment for perfection is not only for our highest good and joy but is also in the highest good and happiness of others.

- *Sit in your usual meditation position.*
- *With both your palms facing upward, lay your right hand on top of your left palm, letting your thumbs touch.*
- *Close your eyes.*
- *Visualize a beautiful sunny day. See the Sun above you, its light rays flickering on the trees and plants around you.*
- *Feel the Sun's warmth and radiance touch your face.*

In front of you stands a Buddhist temple. You take the steps leading up to the temple's entrance and go inside. As you walk in, you can smell the incense in the air. A sense of peace and tranquility comes over you. At the end of the temple stands a magnificent golden statue of Buddha.

- *Walk toward the Buddha statue, and bow to him with your hands in prayer position.*
- *Sit down in front of him.*

- *You begin to observe the figure of Buddha in great detail, taking as long as you need to do so.*
- *Firstly, gaze at his face and look into his eyes.*
- *Observe his joyful smile and his large ears and earlobes.*
- *Next, start to explore Buddha's body. Look at his chest; look at his robe and the all the creases and folds in it.*
- *Look at his arms, his divine upright body, his right hand placed in his left palm, and his thumbs touching to make the shape of a triangle.*
- *Keep exploring the rest of his flawless being, including his legs, feet, and toes, and any other details of Buddha that catch your eye.*
- *See his perfection.*
- *Now take your awareness to the top of his head. A thousand-petal lotus flower begins to blossom at his crown.*
- *See rays of light start to radiate out from the top of his head, enveloping the Buddha's form and the space around him. The image of Buddha and this light begins to resonate deep within you.*
- *Receive any spiritual insights from being in the presence of Buddha.*
- *Continue to take all the time that you need to enjoy this space while still concentrating on this deity's joy and beauty.*
- *When you are ready, imagine standing up and bowing to Buddha with your hands in prayer position.*
- *Thank him for the many blessings and insights that he has bestowed on you today.*
- *Take a deep breath, and then open your eyes.*

Further Guidance

Contemplate or write down the insights and experiences that you received from this meditation, integrating any wisdom into your daily life. If you wish, you may adapt this visualization by concentrating on any other self-realized master of your choice.

Step 5

The Healing Power of Forgiveness

As you grow spiritually, you will find yourself becoming more insightful about why others act the way they do, which can make it easier for you to forgive. In this step, you will not only discover how to look at your past in a different light to help you let go and move on but you will also learn how to forgive others and to forgive yourself to clear your energy of old hurts and regrets to bring about a sense of well-being.

Connect with the Present Moment

Being in the now of things disconnects you from your thoughts about your past and future so you feel less mentally and emotionally distracted. It is through being in the present moment that you can forget your struggles from long ago and break free of old unhelpful patterns, giving you the chance to think and act in new and higher ways. In fact, it is through consciously touching on the present moment that you can reach a higher space, where realizations into the nature of Supreme Spirit can be experienced. This next meditation is especially beneficial to do after meditating on the light or when used as a type of meditation on its own.

Meditation: Experiencing the Present Moment

Take some quiet time somewhere where you will not be disturbed.

- *Take several slow deep breaths and relax.*
- *Refrain from tainting this quiet time with thoughts about your day or life.*
- *Sit still and quiet, taking your time to just look around you.*
- *Try to find something beautiful or agreeable to look at, and go within, appreciating that object for a while.*
- *Now focus outward as if you aren't looking at anything specific but taking in the whole scene in front of you.*
- *As you do so, see if you can touch on an inherent energy behind all that you see. Take your time doing this.*

How do you experience this energy? How does it make you feel?

- *Feel this energy or higher consciousness awaken you.*

Life Can Be Your Greatest Teacher

Life gives us a constant moment-to-moment opportunity to awake to Supreme Spirit and to self-realize the soul's light. If you are aware of what is happening around you and the higher reason as to why it is, you can then choose to come from a higher stance or not. For instance, you can choose to be uncaring and cold toward others or act in a more evolved way, such as gentle and understanding. Or you could take a situation that you find difficult to handle and call it all bad, not realizing that a blessing will exist within it. As you evolve spiritually, do not miss those everyday opportunities that are encouraging you to know and be your truth.

Accept Yourself and Your Life

Everything in your life up till now has been perfect to help you recall who you truly are and who you are not. Try not to fight against yourself and your life by telling yourself that it is or was all wrong. For various reasons, you have created your life as it is up to this point, and you may like who and where you are or not. If you find yourself in the position of the latter, then accepting yourself and all that has happened in your life up to this moment will serve you in moving on and starting anew.

You can free your past by letting go of any unhappy past events that tend to trouble your mind and emotions. Refrain from mulling over those long-past hard years, as they can pull you down and go out to attract more of what you do not want. Regrets of what could have been can also stop you from living fully now, blinding you from appreciating your current gifts and joys that can make you feel content today. And if you keep concentrating on what is wrong in your life, then those areas that were working can start to fall apart.

If you do choose to think about the past, learn to only reminisce on the rosier years when you were successful, loved, and content, as these happier memories can encourage upbeat emotions within you to help create a more positive life. Looking back on happier former years can make you feel good, yet when you think of happy times with loved ones who have passed away, these memories can sometimes make you feel nostalgic and sad because you feel that those people are no longer with you.

Of course, believing in life after death can be comforting, as you know you will eventually be reunited with your beloveds when you pass away. Or if reincarnation rings true for you, you could look forward to the fact that you may well have future lives and more pleasurable times with these temporarily departed souls. Actually, your much-loved deceased are never far away from you, and just the mere thought of them can bring their spiritual presence to you. As your vibration continues to rise, the presence and love of your dearly departed can be sensed around you quite naturally.

Understanding Your Past Will Help Set It Free

Try to see something positive in the negative. There are positive reasons for your earlier years, as you would not be who you are today without them. For example, seeing where you did not receive much affection as a child may have made you more committed to loving yourself or made you decide to bring up your children with more warmth and care. Because of a challenging adverse time, you may have changed your life direction for the better. Or perhaps this time pushed you to believe in yourself and your dreams, something that, until then, you always had difficulty in doing.

What positive outcome has your history made you realize? Seeing some good that came out of your bygone years can definitely help change the way you react to the past. However, if situations from long ago are still troubling you, then forgiveness can help you release the old and heal yourself.

Forgiveness Liberates the Soul

For some of us, it is easy to be this soulful way, yet for others, it is something that we do not really want to do. However, you will feel lighter through the act of forgiveness as it frees destructive energy such as resentment and anger held within your being to bring about improved mental, emotional, and physical health. Also, holding on to a grudge sits within your aura, which unfortunately only attracts more of the same negativity. Therefore, the act of forgiveness can help clear you of negative energy.

Indeed, when you forgive another or yourself, you are in fact loving yourself. You are saying that you now accept what happened but you no longer want to feel annoyed, hurt, or disappointed anymore, and you want to feel better. Is there any part of you feeling sore or out of balance because of holding on to an old grudge? Is there anyone you could forgive to bring about a sense of well-being? Releasing these heavy feelings through forgiveness can be wholesome and healing, and it will soften your energy.

Example Scenario

Mary was a wife who felt very disappointed in her husband, Jack, for not working hard enough to support her and their children in his younger years, and she began to feel very bitter that they had less financial security than she had expected to have when they retired. Her resentment toward him about this issue began to express itself as a continual moaning and outbursts of anger at him. In fact, he could never do right, even though in his later years, he worked harder and had mellowed somewhat. Mary decided to look at how she really felt and then took steps to forgive her husband. On reflection, she soon realized that she not only needed to forgive Jack but she needed to forgive herself for not being strong enough with her husband in her younger years.

Within days after forgiving him and herself, she was amazed at how their relationship began to take on a whole new footing. A newfound harmony entered their marriage, and even certain ailments that had troubled her for years began to clear up.

A release of negative energy can be felt after forgiving someone, making you feel a lot lighter, brighter, and well, not to mention that it can improve your relationships. Forgiveness not only stops you from attracting similar painful situations in the future, but it can also help free the people you are forgiving from their pasts too, thus giving them an opportunity to act in better ways.

Be Compassionate and Understanding with Yourself

Before forgiving someone, begin by understanding how you felt about a past upsetting matter. Not that you have to sit for weeks or months dwelling on an issue — as this can be detrimental to your sense of well-being — but until you pull out a constantly niggling past incident from your mind and take a really good look at how you feel about it, it may not be easy to forgive another.

Acknowledging your feelings can sometimes be tricky. At times, we do not want to bring up the hurt or disappointment we feel because we are afraid that it will be too overwhelming and upsetting. Also, we are brought up to feel this and to not feel that — to not cry, not show our anger, and not feel hurt or vulnerable. As children, we can stop ourselves from feeling pain or distress to help survive upsetting times, and then we can block our true feelings about what happened by going emotionally numb. Then we can find ourselves having grown up without even knowing how we truly feel, until one day we get seriously ill, have a serious accident, or depression sets in out of the blue. Also, teachings from our parents or society on how we ought to feel can mix us up; for example, when a child freely expresses herself with joy but is severely reprimanded by a parent for doing so, she will grow up feeling that it is bad to be happy and so finds it hard to allow herself to let go and be happy in adult life.

If you want to forgive someone, you will need to look at how you feel about what happened. Do not give yourself a hard time or question why you feel a certain way; just let your feelings rise up and accept them unconditionally. It is by being compassionate and understanding with yourself that you can be more understanding about where this other person was coming from who you would now like to forgive.

There may be many reasons why another would choose to act in a certain way. Assess the situation and consider all the options. Maybe this person you felt offended by felt threatened or scared in some way? Perhaps this person felt jealous or inferior to you or experienced the same thing as what he or she did to you? Could this person have been ill at the time and not thinking straight? Was the wrongdoer's upbringing short of education and love that then led him or her to act in lesser ways?

Getting an understanding of why that person displeased you can prevent you from feeling so hurt and angry. This is not to say that what this person did was all right. Deliberately hurting or being inconsiderate, insensitive, or cruel are not evolved ways of being. In fact, in the long run, you would be only hurting yourself by doing such acts; what goes around comes around. However, looking at why some people would have chosen to act the way they did can make you aware of others' levels of evolution, making it easier for you to detach and to let go.

Once you have forgiven those in question, it does not mean that you have to spend time with them or try to become best buddies — unless, of course, you have a true desire to do so. Your feelings about these people may have changed through your understanding and forgiving them but their reactions to you may not. Therefore, unless the people you forgave understand and respect your feelings on this issue and are willing to make a genuine change in the way they are with you, it would probably be best not to put yourself in their company. However, as forgiveness can bring about inner peace, you may now feel that you do not need others as a certain way for you to feel good about yourself.

Your true nature is love, so it is natural to want to express your love and be loved. When you look more deeply at another soul who has upset you, it is not the fact that you actually dislike this other soul, for you know that intrinsically this soul is love. It means that you dislike the person's actions.

By comparing another's actions to your own, you can at least assist yourself in knowing your level of evolution. Someone may have acted in heartless ways, yet by comparison, you know that you would have probably acted in a much higher way. Seeing the levels of evolution of people through their actions can at least help you know your level of development and who you are to make you feel better.

If you feel bothered by something that someone did to you and you are having trouble moving on, take some quiet time and send that person forgiveness to help bring yourself relief of the situation.

Visualization: the Sacred Heart of Jesus Christ

The beloved Jesus Christ said, "Father forgive them for they know not what they do" [Luke 23:34, KJV] while being crucified on the cross — a prime example of a high level of forgiveness and compassion. This meditation uses the image of Jesus Christ to help you forgive another, but you may choose any other enlightened figure you wish.

- *Close your eyes and sit in your usual meditation posture.*

- *Take some deep breaths in, letting go of any bodily tension as you breathe out.*
- *Feel yourself becoming very relaxed.*
- *Go deep within and imagine that you are sitting in a pillar of white light.*
- *Feel centered and emotionally calm within this light.*

We call on the great spiritual master, Jesus Christ, to help radiate the energies of love, clarity, and forgiveness.

- *Picture him now and look into his eyes.*
- *Feel a comforting, unconditional love from his presence.*
- *Look at the area around his heart chakra.*

A golden and white light is shining from his chest. The light from Christ's heart chakra begins to resonate with your heart chakra, helping you to open your heart and soften your energy with love.

- *Take yourself back to an event that has been troubling you.*
- *See the people involved who caused you upset or pain.*

How old were you? Where were you? What happened?

- *See this past scene fully.*
- *Acknowledge all your feelings about this issue.*

Where do you feel this upset in your body? You may feel the need to reflect on what happened, how you felt then, and how you feel now about the issue. You can stop the CD now and continue playing this visualization when you are ready.

- *Turn your focus to the person involved in this event that you need to forgive.*

Can you see fear in this person? Weakness? A feeling of inferiority or even vulnerability? Can you see the person's level of evolution at that time? Why do you think this person offended you? Could it be that what happened was not meant to hurt you. It is here that Christ's light will help you see with clarity whatever you need to understand about this past situation.

- *Take your time now to receive wisdom and insights on this issue. Are you ready to forgive this person?*
- *If you feel that you are, tell this person from your heart that you now forgive him or her.*

- *As you do so, you release any negative feelings toward this person, and your aura is cleared and healed from this act of forgiveness.*
- *Sense that person and the images of this past issue now being released from your mind, body, and emotions.*

How do you feel after forgiving this person?

- *See yourself as a winner of this past circumstance by finding something positive to come of it.*

Maybe you learned who your friends were in times of need; you realized a soul quality within yourself such as self-respect, clarity, or strength; or you changed your life direction for the better. Perhaps you now have greater empathy for others who have experienced a similar situation to yours and are now available to give those people valuable help and support. Or it is possible that you just needed to remember the event in order to forgive. What good thing came out of this upsetting time for you?

- *Finally, thank the enlightened presence of Jesus Christ for helping you today.*
- *Come back into the room with peace in your heart, ready to start anew.*

Further Guidance

Over the next few days, allow your higher self to gently show you other people you could forgive to help clear yourself of negative energy. These people or incidents may come to mind in the following days or weeks ahead. As they do, give yourself the necessary time and space to run the above meditation for each person and sense your energy free up and become lighter.

Forgive Yourself

You may be cross with another, yet if you look more closely, perhaps you are angry at yourself. Looking back, you may see that you could have been wiser, stronger, or more loving with yourself or with others.

For a sense of well-being, learn to drop any debilitating feelings of guilt about what you did in the past by forgiving yourself. You are also in the process of maturing and remembering to be more of your soul's light. Who you were years ago is not necessarily who you are now. It might be that you have progressed a lot since then, and you probably understand better ways of being. Do you have any regrets about how you behaved in the past? Maybe now is the time to apologize to those you feel you let down and forgive yourself.

Visualization: Apologizing

It is very important that you do your utmost to amend any regretful situation by acting in higher and more responsible ways that respect the person in question. If this is not possible or if you are no longer in contact with him or her, this next visualization can help you make amends with the person you feel you upset in the past.

- *Go within and connect with the light at your third eye.*
- *See a radiant sun above you, and let its light rays touch and illuminate you.*
- *Feel truly loved in this focus of light.*
- *Start to envision the person you let down in the past.*
- *See yourself lovingly greet this person.*
- *Take your time to express to this person how much you appreciated him or her.*
- *Tell this person how much you liked or loved him or her.*
- *Explain to the person that you now know what he or she must have been feeling at that time and why he or she might have felt upset, hurt, or let down by the way you acted toward them.*
- *While sending this person love from your heart, apologize to him or her.*
- *Share with this person that you have seen a more evolved way of being.*
- *Make an inner commitment to yourself that if you are ever in a similar situation again, you will act in a more loving, wise, evolved way.*
- *Finally, place your right hand over your heart, and lovingly forgive yourself.*

Further Guidance

Remember that there is always a higher reason why things happen as they do. Everything that you or someone else has done has, in its mysterious way, assisted another, even if it did not look like it at the time. Try to see the perfection in it all and remember: There is no such thing as an accident in life.

Step 6
Evolving with Love and Light

As you accomplish your dreams, life's work, and higher purpose, you may well find yourself coming up against self-doubts, negative blocks, or old ways of thinking and being, which can hinder you from creating the life you want and stop you from being more of your true self. These unhelpful aspects of you represent parts of your less-than-positive personality, your shadows within, that need to be recognized and shown a more developed way of being to represent more of your higher self and to support you in achieving your goals.

These unsupportive parts of your persona may have come about from outdated beliefs that you were told by your family, friends, or society that you took on as true when you were younger and that still influence you today. You may hold negative attitudes that you brought into this life from a past one. Or because of a problematic time when you were younger, you may have chosen to see yourself in a negative light or view life as a constant struggle and hardship. In addition to these, your less-evolved personalities may show up as patterns or habits that are not beneficial to your sense of well-being and growth, that stop you from being balanced, or that keep you from feeling good about yourself. They can even reveal themselves as destructive behaviors like overeating, drug abuse, and alcoholism.

Your personality is made up of many subpersonalities, like separate characters in a play who determine the way you think, act, and create.

Some of these are what you would call good or positive aspects of you—thoughts and ways that assist you in being and expressing more of your truth, like being optimistic, patient, or compassionate. Yet lurking in the shadows, you may possess uncooperative ideas about yourself that do not help you reach your full potential.

For example, if you were raised in an environment of much poverty and hardship, there may be an old part of you that still believes there is not enough and that you have to work long, hard hours to just get by. The personality that thinks, "There is never enough" or "I can only make money if I work really hard in a job that I do not like" will then need to be recognized and reprogrammed into a higher way of thinking to help make your life easier. Or because of a past unhappy relationship with an ex-partner, whispers in the back of your mind may project a lack of confidence and self-worth in finding that special mate.

Meditations: Four Steps to Transform the Negative into the Positive

No individual being is or can ever be intrinsically bad. The truth of each being is bright, loving, and positive beyond measure; however, many of you have forgotten your wonderful truth through the illusions of such negative dross. On the path of self-development, it is essential to become aware of where you are coming from and decide whether your thoughts and actions are lending a hand at creating your heaven on earth or not. Then steps can be taken to integrate each hindering part of your personality into a higher way of thinking and being that is more in line with your true nature and can help create the life you desire.

Step One: Become Aware of Your Negativity

To begin with, you will need to recognize a less-evolved part of your personality. This might feel a little uncomfortable at first because your lower self that has less light does not like to be changed, and many of us do not like to admit our unhelpful or less-progressive ways. Yet only by being awake and honest with how you are thinking and being can you begin to let the light in to positively change these uncooperative illusions.

- *Sit up straight in a meditation position.*
- *Connect with the light at the third eye.*
- *See this light now shine down around you.*

- *Imagine that you are sitting as your higher self.*
- *Ask the light to now show you any part of your personality that could evolve. Perhaps you already know what part of you needs evolving.*
- *See this personality now appear in front of you as a separate character. What does it look like?*

Step Two: Get to Know This Less-Evolved Side of You

The next step in positively reprogramming any uncooperative personality is not to make this part of you wrong, because maybe you set it up in the past to assist you in some positive way. It could be that a fear of moving forward into new arenas is actually trying to protect you, or perhaps you do not have a clear idea of what you are trying to create. Maybe a side of you that is afraid of failing, scared of getting hurt, or impatient to reach your goal has a sound reason why it is this way. Your job will not be to fight against this personality, but to accept it unconditionally.

- *Ask this part of your personality why it is being this way and listen to what it has to say.*
- *Tell it that it is unconditionally loved by you.*
- *Express that you now understand what it is trying to do but would like its help. Ask it if it would be willing to change the way it thinks or acts into a more evolved way of being that will help you be who you want to become and do what you want to accomplish.*

Step Three: Get Clear on Who You Choose to Be and What You Want to Create

Any part of your persona that you are trying to evolve will need to know what you are working toward. For example, say your vision is to own your own business but a little voice inside you says that you lack talent at managing your own company. Even though you have much experience at helping run someone else's business, a personality within you still doubts that you would be capable in achieving this goal successfully.

To help realize your dream of running your own business, you will have to show those less-than-capable personalities ideas and pictures of what you are aiming for. To motivate yourself to become slim and healthy, you will need to present to that part of you that sees yourself as unmotivated and overweight a vision of you at your ideal weight. To positively transform that aspect of you that has trouble believing you can attain enlightenment, you will need a clear image of you being more of your higher self.

What is your dream or vision? Who do you want to be? Be clear on who you choose to be and what you want to create, and then stick to those goals, as continually changing your mind about your aims can be confusing and unproductive to the personality.

- *Tell this personality who you want to be and what you want to create.*
- *Show the personality a clear vision of what you want.*

Step Four: Transform Your Personality with Love and Light

After showing this personality what you are heading for, request that it now cooperates with you. Ask this personality if it would be willing to drop the old patterns and thoughts for a more positive outlook and way that will support you in fulfilling your ambitions. If this old personality now agrees to this higher change, then now is the time to call on the divine love and light to help you.

- *See this light like a spiritual sun shining its light onto this personality and let that light now surround it. See this personality broadcast a focus of love and light to help bring about a smooth and positive transformation.*
- *Wait a while until a new and evolved personality appears. How does it look now?*
- *What new and higher belief does this transformed personality now hold? Hear from this transformed personality now.*
- *Let this newly re-formed personality now merge with you under a focus of light from the spiritual sun.*

Balancing the Negative and the Positive

They say that there are always two sides to a story, and when it comes to your personality, there is no exception. We live in the world of duality, so if a positive personality exists within you, then the opposing side could be presenting itself too.

Example Scenario

In her heart, Mandy always wanted to be happily married and have a couple of children. However, in her younger years, she saw her parents always arguing, and her much older brother — who was also married — did not seem contentedly married, either. It was through seeing other people's marriages fall apart that Mandy also decided that marriage was not for her. Later in life, when it came to committing herself to someone she deeply loved, these two opposing personalities — one that believed in marriage and one that did not — fought within her, and she was unable to make a decision about whether to get married.

You might be very health conscious and fit, but within you lies an identity that does not want to give up smoking, which you know is not good for you. Mystically, you might know yourself as a spiritually developed being with much insight, awareness, and light; nonetheless, you have a side that has trouble accepting and believing in your spiritual side that makes you hide your light under a bushel.

Taking the last example, perhaps that aspect of you that does not fully believe in your level of spirituality came about when you were very young. Perchance your family or friends were not aware of your spiritual development, or maybe they even tried to put you down for thinking or acting in such unfamiliar ways. Perhaps you decided to hold yourself back from expressing and believing in your light so as not to upset and make those around you feel insecure and to be more accepted by those nearest and dearest to you. As you become more aware of how you think and act, you will realize that even those less-accommodating sides of you are in fact not your enemies but your friends, trying to protect you or bring you love. Can you recognize any two contrasting beliefs within you that seem to go against each other?

Visualization: Harmonizing Conflicting Personalities

- *Sit in your usual meditation posture.*
- *Bring to mind two contradictory parts of your personality that you would like to bring into balance.*

  What is each one saying? Do they have different images?
- *Tell both of these personalities what you would like from them. Ask them whether they would be willing to come to a compromise to harmoniously work together to help you achieve your goals and highest good.*
- *If they both agree to help you, call on the light of your higher self.*

- *See your higher self as an angel of light.*
- *Picture this angel enveloping these two opposing parts of your personality with embracing wings of light.*

Love and light is broadcasted to positively unite these two sides of your personality to work together harmoniously as one. Wait until the wings of your angel open to reveal just one balanced, developed, and inspired personality. This new image of your personality now becomes clear.

- *Listen to anything it has to say, any insights about how it is going to help you.*
- *Lastly, visualize the wings of this angel embracing you and this harmonized personality, letting the two of you merge in a hub of love and light.*

Be Aware of Your Fears

Behind anger, worry, or anxiety, you will find fear. You can bet that if there is negativity somewhere within you, then fear is the culprit. As you become more self-aware, you will come to uncover your underlying fears, the roots to your problems, which motivate you to think, say, or act in less-helpful ways. When you come from fear, you are acting from your less-evolved self, a place of little love, trust, and optimism. Fear is the less-developed reason for doing things and will always hold you back from self-fulfillment, inhibiting you from knowing that life is actually looking after you. Fear, worry, and insecurity not only hamper your sense of well-being, but when you come to dread something enough, you will begin to attract this fearful situation into your life as thought begins to create your reality.

Know the difference between being fearful and being cautious. Fears are illusionary, something that you have made up at some time. Being cautious, on the other hand, means being observant and alert to what's going on around you and aware of what your feelings and intuition are saying. Cautiousness is the more intelligent and sound way to take care of yourself, your loved ones, and the planet, and it represents a higher way in comparison to fear.

What could be the more evolved reason for doing things? Love. Love will encourage you to grow and be who you really are to benefit your life and others. Maybe there is a side to you that is a perfectionist, scared that if you fail you will not be accepted by others. Or perhaps you have a workaholic side that can never stop for long, because if you do, you will uncover an uncomfortable emptiness inside that needs to be healed. What motivates you? Is it fear or love?

Visualization: Insight from a Master

- *Sit up with your spine straight, shoulders relaxed, and eyes closed.*

You are standing in the most beautiful and lush garden, surrounded by an array of diverse plants and opulent nature where every tree and flower is an image of perfection. This is a truly heavenly place. An enlightened master is standing next to you, appreciating the depth of color and fragrance of some flowers. Flowers represent a blossoming of perfection.

- *As this master turns to you, see a glistening light in his or her eyes and feel an unconditional love.*
- *See the master offer you one of these special flowers.*
- *Place this flower in your heart.*

The master has come here to help you become aware of a fear, negative belief, or block you are unconsciously holding that is keeping you from accomplishing your higher purpose or stopping you from being your truth and living the life you want. The master is going to enlighten you about this.

It is here that you will start to receive pictures or scenes that reveal where this negativity originally came from. Take all the time you need to receive these insights. Do you understand how this thought came about? Is it from your childhood or from a past life? Is it from the pool of collective consciousness that many people are living in? Listen to anything else that this great one has to say. What new and positive thought do you need to believe to help you progress?

- *Say that positive belief to yourself three times.*
- *Take a moment and imagine yourself being this new way.*
- *The master touches your heart, sending a powerful transmission of love and light to help break down the illusion.*
- *Feel a lightness within.*
- *Thank this special, enlightened master for assisting you.*
- *Open your eyes, and come back fully into the room, feeling renewed, vibrant, and wide-awake.*

Further Guidance

Keep this new positive outlook in mind and affirm it to yourself daily. In the next day or so, after doing any of the above meditations, you will begin to notice an encouraging and positive difference in this area of your personality. It is important that you continue to use the above visualizations — the four steps to transform the negative into the positive — to help evolve any parts of your negative personality along your path of ascension. The more you transform your unhelpful personalities to positively support you, the more you will become your higher self and achieve what you are really capable of.

Step 7
Realizing Your Life's Purpose

Everyone has a purpose, a soul reason for being on Earth. The work that you do will not only benefit your sense of well-being but in the process, it will assist those around you, humanity, or the planet in some positive way.

Your Life's Work Will Be Something You Love to Do

To begin to know what you are here to do, you first need to believe that you have a special contribution to make. Each one of you is like an individual snowflake, uniquely reflecting your light and beauty out into the world. And your life's work will be something special and distinctive, something that you enjoy doing and that will help you to grow. Your life purpose is not something that someone or society tells you would be good or worthy. It is something that really inspires and motivates you, a heartfelt desire to be and do.

Maybe your purpose is being at home with your children — bringing them up with much care and tolerance, teaching them how to be responsible, loving, and honest human beings who will help bring about their full potential and yours. Your preference might be assisting others to open up to new and higher ways of thinking and doing things in your specified profession and work environment. Or your priority might be to develop spiritually and radiate a feeling of serenity, inner peace, and light. Whether you are working in business, finance, teaching, education, healing, medicine, the environment, plants, animals, the arts, writing, or something else, you will have an individual contribution to make if you are enlightening, as your vibration will affect those around you without you having to say or teach anything.

Your life's purpose can give you the opportunity to be your higher nature. Two people may have the same job and responsibilities, but the way they carry them out might be poles apart. For instance, take the jobs of two fathers. One looks after his children with much shown affection and gives them the necessary attention and time, which he greatly takes pleasure in; the other generally reacts to his children in an impatient manner and forgets to see the importance in participating in their education and having fun with the family. Both fathers are doing the same job, yet the former is coming from a level of love and responsibility that represents a more evolved way of being. Therefore, it is not what you do but how you do it that is most vital to your self-development and the good of others. Whatever mundane work or act you undertake, you can make it become your higher purpose if you so choose.

Live in higher purpose. Higher purpose is about balancing your energies, healing yourself, and expressing your light out into the world in your own exceptional way. As you raise your vibration, grow spiritually, and serve humanity or the planet in some special way, you will be living in higher purpose and thus feel fulfilled.

Consciously aim to be more of your higher self in whatever you undertake to help realize your truth. Giving your best in whatever you do, loving your life and honoring all other life, creating a place of beauty, loving yourself, and being understanding, kind, and compassionate to yourself and others can suggest that you are coming from higher purpose. Anytime you experience and express yourself as peace, love, strength, joy, intuition, clarity, responsibility, wisdom, beauty, compassion, patience, love, light, service, and kindness, you are expressing more of your soul's light and are accomplishing your higher purpose.

Meditation: Soul Agenda

Do you know which qualities of your higher self you are presently working with?

- *Sit in your quiet and undisturbed place of meditation.*
- *Take some deep breaths and relax.*
- *Breathe normally.*

- *Start to make or sing some harmonious and lovely sounds. Just let these beautiful sounds come out naturally.*
- *Continue to sing your note and special sounds for the next five minutes or so. [Pause.]*
- *Stop making these sounds, and look up and out through your third eye, connecting with the light.*
- *See this light beam down all around you.*
- *Feel complete and loved in this focus of light.*
- *Ask what higher ways of being you should currently be working on to experience and express in your life.*
- *Inquire if there is anything you can do to become closer to this higher attribute?*
- *Imagine and feel yourself being this way now.*
- *Finally, commit to putting any of your insight into action.*

The Greatest Gift You Can Give Another Is to Make Your Own Life Work

To gear you into the direction of self-fulfillment, allow yourself to listen to the whispers of your heart about what your special path is, spending time to relax and daydream about who you want to be. Visualize yourself, step by step, accomplishing your desired work. Refrain from letting doubts enter your mind by telling you who you cannot be. Get quiet and relaxed and receive visions and feelings sent from your higher self of what you are here to do. Also, see that what you are here to do will benefit others.

When you are willing to believe that you have some special part to play and are open to doing it, your life's work will begin to unfold. It will be work that really inspires and motivates you, an activity that you get real pleasure from doing and that you can easily focus on and be self-disciplined to do. You will always make the time to do your life's work, and that time can seem to fly by with a feeling as if you are at one and in the flow of things.

Some of you may worry that you do not have the necessary skills to carry out your work, yet if you were to look within and were honest with yourselves, you would know that you do in fact possess in-born talents and abilities that perhaps you have not fully acknowledged or fully expressed yet. In the initial stages of opening to your work, your angels

— in the form of supportive friends, family, and your spiritual guides — may also encourage you to get on your path, suggesting new avenues to explore or new skills to develop.

Of course, there is the question of recourses. If you are carrying out your life's work, will you be given enough time, help, and money to get your project going? Actually, many a time it is not actually a question of money that stops you from doing your chosen work but a lack of belief in yourself and the good that you can create. Fears of success and failure within you will need to be talked to, showing them a vision of exactly what you are aiming for. Many of you who have not even begun to realize your specialty may say, "Who am I to think I am so talented and able?" By not recognizing your gifts and dreams, you are denying who you are and stopping yourself from feeling fulfilled.

Respect your path and the life paths of others. Be clear on what enlivens you in life — not what others want from you or want you to live up to. Those who love you the most can sometimes be the real culprits in holding you back. This is usually because as you spend more time doing what makes you feel good, those closest to you may feel that you will have less time for them. If anyone is making you feel guilty for not seeing them enough or is pulling on you for attention, yet deep down you feel that you really don't have the time to give, you may need to change the relationship to suit your needs

Visualization: Affirming Your Path

- *Visualize yourself surrounded by a column of light. See yourself centered, standing in your own power in this shining light.*
- *Bring into view the person you feel is either trying to consume your time or is keeping you away from your life's work.*
- *Send this person love from your heart, and wish the person happiness.*
- *Tell this person telepathically that you need to spend more time doing the things that bring you joy and the things that are important to you. This includes your life's work.*
- *Tell this person about the very important activities you need to focus on.*
- *Ask for the higher self of this person to come forward.*
- *Ask this person to turn to his or her higher self.*
- *See this person being embraced by the light of his or her higher self.*

- *Let the higher self of this person show him or her what is in the highest good for this person to spend time on that will also bring joy to him or her.*
- *Thank this person for understanding your current needs and for working with you.*
- *Come back into the room feeling light and free to do what is in your highest good.*
- *Notice the difference in the way this person behaves with you in the next few days and weeks ahead.*

On the path of ascension, your thoughts about yourself and life will evolve, and these could challenge those nearest to you, especially if they are stuck in old, less-evolved ways of being. Others may try to put down what you believe in, kick up a fuss, or even create situations that subtly try to stop you from accomplishing your highest good, yet sometimes these situations are necessary to help you believe in yourself and your dreams.

However, nobody can own another human being, whether that person is part of your family or not. You are all free spirits, and that is how you need to feel — free to do what brings out your joy. Anyone possessive or controlling who tries to stop you from doing what you enjoy needs to understand that if it is in your highest good to undertake something, then it will most certainly benefit that person in the long run too. Whatever happens, do not discontinue doing what you love because of the less heartening reactions of others; otherwise, you will slow down your growth, only to feel resentful later on in life for not following your heart.

Whether it is with your neighbors, friends, or family, refrain from comparing your life with what another has and does, and stop putting yourself in competition with others. No one is — nor can one ever be — better than anyone else. The successful director is no better than the person who cleans the streets. Both are equal in spirit, each one evolving in one's own special way at one's own special pace to know who he or she truly is. It could be that the road sweeper's capacity to be of service to the community, to live joyfully with faith and trust in Supreme Spirit, is highly developed. He may live his life with a respectful and gentle attitude toward others, something that perhaps an egocentric and greedy top dog might not have yet progressed to.

The highly accomplished do not judge others for the type of work that they do, never feeling superior among the toilet cleaners or inferior among the high powered in this world (or vice versa). Each one of you has a part to play and is a part of the one Spirit, equal and undivided in essence and made in the image of the one maker. It is through the gift of life that all souls are given a chance to remember and express who they truly are through carrying out their life's work.

Time Is on Your Side

Let go of current collective thought forms that say you must realize or achieve your life's work by a certain young age or else you will not make it or be a failure. This idea only contributes to making you feel pressured to accomplish your goals in this certain amount of time you have. Many of those who are bringing new thought forms, teaching, and healing do not come into their own until they have been through some important life experiences and have reached forty or much older. If you are coming from higher purpose, you will have all the time you need to achieve what you are here to do.

Your life's purpose could take time to fully realize. In the process of knowing and making it real, you may need to learn new talents, recognize more about who you are, and mature, so learn to be patient with yourself and trust in Supreme Spirit to get there. There is a right time for everything. Your life's work will be something that you cannot push to make happen, but with time, faith, and some effort, life will get you there at your own pace and when you are ready.

See Supreme Spirit as Your Employer and Wage Giver

It is Supreme Spirit who is our benevolent giver, who supports us with money, people, or whatever we need to start and continue our work. Spirit's help and wherewithal will come through other people, resources, and new opportunities, so be open and grateful for whatever comes your way to help you achieve your goal.

Once you have sent out a clear request that you are ready and willing to begin doing what you love, situations, people, opportunities, and training will begin to arrive to get you in line to accomplish it. Be receptive to new ways of having things — maybe going down different avenues that you have not thought about before — and be open to meeting new people who will assist you in manifesting your work. Stay alert to new opportunities that unexpectedly pop up and are related to your work. Do not pass them up when they arrive.

As you meditate, look out of your third eye to the image of light and keep your concentration fixed on this area between your eyebrows. Talk to the Supreme Spirit here and ask for assistance to start and accomplish your particular work, all the time listening to your feelings and intuition on the right action to take. Listen to your spirit guides and masters too, keeping an open channel with them to allow them to come in.

You Are Always Free to Choose What You Want to Do and Be

Before you were born, you chose to be with or meet up with certain people in this lifetime, setting up certain landmarks, people, and circumstances to help you accomplish your goals and purpose. From then on, you have always been free to choose what you want to do, yet your heartfelt desires and dreams will point you in the direction toward self-fulfillment.

Nonetheless, big or small, you may have setbacks along the way to accomplishing your work. The trick here is not to see them as setbacks. Perhaps you are learning to develop your patience or trust when things do not seem to go smoothly. Maybe whatever is slowing you down is making you even more determined to reach your goal, or it could be that a hold-up is actually a way that Supreme Spirit is looking after you in some way.

If the road gets a little bit bumpy, the trick is not to let what comes in front of you unbalance or dishearten you. Try to overcome what hinders you by not dwelling on the issue but take positive action wherever necessary. Pray to the light for help and keep listening to your wise intuition for a solution, only then take action. The more you get upset in the face of a hitch, the more it can become a crisis. Resolve any problems as calmly as you can, as if you are not letting them become difficulties. Remember, you are the one who has power over your obstacles, not vice versa. And you can ask the divine for help.

If life were too easy, we would never feel that we are growing, not noticing a sense of satisfaction when we do achieve something worthwhile. People who attain great success usually have to work at it, and long-lasting success rarely comes overnight, although it can once you let Supreme Spirit take over. Even those who wake up to find that they have won a fortune have been getting ready over the years to receive this opportune moment. Keep concentrating on those areas that are working in your life, and look at where you feel looked after and loved. Every day, see the good in your life and say to yourself that you are lucky to keep your spirits high.

Develop Faith and Trust

You may think that you are doing your life's work on your own, but once you commit to doing it, you will start to get help from all sides. Family members or acquaintances may come in with support or other means. Your spiritual guides will also come in with worthy encouragement or advice, and Life (Supreme Spirit) will know of your direction to accomplish your life's work, bringing you the opportunities and circumstances to get you on your way. Realizing you have such remarkable assistance takes away the worry of who, when, where, and what next to help you relax and enjoy the journey.

Trust in Supreme Spirit to make whatever you need come forth to help you accomplish your special work. You may put doubts into your mind about why you are not able to create something or be a success in your specialized field, but this negativity will only hinder you from receiving Spirit's bounty and new possibilities. It is time to let go of those self-conscious fears and doubts and have a go. Your life can be seen as one long experience of many experiences, so there is nothing to lose — only experience to gain. What then, do you want to experience in life?

The most important thing to your soul is that you are evolving and remembering to be who you truly are, and your life's work can help you achieve that. Being a divine spark, you have within you the ability to create a life you love, your higher purpose, and much good.

Visualization: Link Yourself to Your Life's Work

- *Lie down on your back, and get comfortable with your arms and legs relaxed by your sides. If necessary, keep yourself warm with a wool or cotton blanket.*
- *Take a deep breath in, and imagine that you are breathing light into your body from a great spiritual sun above you.*
- *As you breathe out, feel yourself letting go and relaxing deeply.*

- *Breathe normally now.*
- *See yourself standing in an open field. Look around you and appreciate the grasses and the colors of wildflowers that are moving in the breeze.*
- *Smell the fragrance of these blossoms; hear the sound of the grass moving gently in the wind and the birds singing.*
- *Feel completely at peace.*
- *See yourself opening your arms to the sky, and see the big smile on your face.*

You are about to open up to what you are here to do.

- *Look up toward the clear, blue sky and bright, golden sun, and take a while to feel this sun radiate warmth and light out to you.*
- *You see a ball of light coming toward you from out of the sky.*
- *See yourself catching this ball in your hands.*

This sphere of light represents your life's work.

- *As you hold it, look at it closely. Take your time to see if it reflects any colors, symbols, or pictures.*
- *Take this radiant ball of light and place it into the area of your heart chakra in the middle of your chest.*

This ball of light starts to resonate with you to help you awaken to your life's work and purpose.

- *See this radiant ball move down to your base chakra.*

Your life purpose is now being earthed. This will aid you in becoming secure and stable in carrying out your life's work.

- *Your unique ball of light moves up to your sacral chakra. Sense a feeling of self-confidence and well-being that will come from doing your life's work.*
- *Next, see your ball of light move up to your solar plexus chakra to motivate you in doing what you came here to do. Feel joy in knowing that you have a special contribution to make, sensing a new drive and willpower to accomplish your life's work.*
- *Rising up to your heart chakra, this ball of light begins to link you with what you love to do that relates to your life's work. It is here that you may receive more visions or images about your higher path. Receive these insights now.*

- *Next, see this radiant ball move up to your throat chakra.*

This sphere of light is activating you to communicate, be creative, and express your purpose. It will also help you to hear your intuitive voice more clearly to guide you in creating what you are here to do.

Lifting up to your brow chakra, your orb of light makes a psychic and intuitive connection to know your life's work and soul's purpose. At this level, you might even begin to see yourself as a teacher, expert, or master in your field.

- *Let this ball of light move into the area of your crown chakra at the top of your head. See your life's work being linked to the will of Supreme Spirit, your soul's dream, and the higher purpose of others.*
- *Let your ball of light move back down to your heart chakra and out between your hands.*
- *Release it into the earth. Watch it go freely wherever it wants to go.*

It may move out and expand into where you are living now and your surrounding area, or it might go far away to different places and even other countries. It could even light up the whole of the world. Wherever it goes is just perfect for you. Do not try to force it or control it in any way. Just watch wherever your light goes.

- *When you are ready, let your ball of light come back to you.*

It has now grown in size and envelops your whole being and the space around you.

- *Feel a sense of fulfillment and joy that comes from doing your special work.*
- *Sit within this sphere of light for a while to assist you in feeling attuned and motivated to carry out your purpose, being attentive to any other insights that come to mind.*
- *Finally, see this ball of light shrink into a much smaller radiant ball, and place it within your heart chakra.*

This will help attract people and opportunities that will assist you in making your life's work real.

- *When you are ready, open your eyes and come back into the room, remembering anything significant.*

Further Guidance

Listen to any urges or feelings about what you would like to do in the days or weeks after doing this visualization. Be awake to any suggestions or encouragement that other people give you that will help you know your path to accomplishing your life's work.

You may feel more energized or inspired to start your special work after doing this visualization, so make use of it when you're feeling tired or uninspired.

Use this visualization whenever you feel that you are diverting from carrying out your life's work or you need extra clarity on the next step of what you are here to do.

Step 8
Awakening to Love

Do you know what is special about you? Stop comparing yourself to others, and acknowledge your own beauty and uniqueness. Whether you are a good parent, an efficient and organized worker, or a kind and giving friend, recognize all those upbeat qualities that you express. When you start to value yourself, you automatically begin to love and believe in yourself. Always appreciate yourself. Right now write a list of all the gifts, talents, and positive attributes that you express. Then get into a new habit of saying them to yourself daily.

Your happiness is extremely important, so for good self-esteem, it is essential that you find out what makes you feel worthy and happy, as this will differ from person to person. Others might have tried to put you down or make you feel bad in the past, usually because they do not acknowledge the good within themselves. For unshakable self-esteem, you will need to believe in yourself without the validation of others, but you do not have to put yourself in the company of those who do not treat you well or honor you. Forgive those who have not respected you in the past and move on to loving yourself.

Love Yourself

The more you love yourself and recognize yourself, the more you will start to attract other people who will want to treat you in the same admiring way. However, it seems that many of you have been taught that you must love others before yourself. This false idea can make you feel unfulfilled and resentful in life, especially if you become so wrapped up in trying to make those around you happy that you forget to nurture your own special needs. If you do not love yourself, then you cannot truly love others, and you might find that others have trouble accepting you, so put loving yourself at the top of your list of priorities. This means loving yourself unconditionally — whatever is happening or however you feel that day. Learn to be compassionate with yourself and to love the inner child within you. If you find someone dishonoring you, you can bet that they do not truly honor themselves.

One of the most important people you can listen to is you. What do you say to yourself? Do you speak to yourself kindly and encouragingly, telling yourself how well you are doing and how wonderful you are? Or do you beat yourself up over every mistake you make and fail to appreciate how far you have come? When you feel low or upset, do you tell yourself that you should not feel this way, and then try to fight or bury your feelings? Loving yourself means understanding and accepting yourself, your actions, and your emotions unconditionally, knowing that you are on a path of ascension and evolving, that you did the best you knew how at the time, and that you are in the process of being lighter and more loving. Any positive and guiding inner messages from your higher self will always speak supportively and wisely to you, so learn to take heed of your inner supportive guru.

Self-worth is another important aspect to loving yourself, and you can start by honoring your feelings. Others may have told you not to feel good about yourself, or you might go over in your mind whether you have real reason to feel disturbed about something that happened to you. Yet if you are already feeling upset, the best thing is to allow and accept how you are feeling, as what you resist will persist. Getting into power struggles and arguments will only close your and the other person's hearts. Instead, learn to be assertive and say no when you do not truly agree with something and to calmly express how you feel. Not that you have to persuade someone to think or feel the same way, but you will need to acknowledge your own feelings to realize your own self-worth.

Loving yourself will always be in your highest good and the highest good for those around you. Those who love themselves tend to be kind, compassionate, and considerate, not selfish and cold to the needs of others. If you remembered your own intrinsic nature, you would know yourself as nothing less than goodness and love. Start each day by telling yourself — with conviction — that you feel good about yourself and love yourself.

Visualization: Love Is in the Air

- *Lie face down on the floor or on a bed.*
- *Lift your arms up so that they are resting by the sides of your head.*
- *Now you are going to relax your whole body.*
- *Begin by letting your feet and toes relax.*
- *Relaxation moves up into your legs, and your hips, and as it does, let any tension here just ooze out from your skin.*
- *Relaxation moves up into your lower and upper back.*
- *Feel the weight of your shoulders drop, and let the muscles in your neck relax.*
- *Let your jaw relax, and let all the muscles in your face relax.*
- *Feel relaxation move down into your chest, arms, and hands and then down into your tummy. Literally feel your body sinking into where you are lying.*
- *Now say, "Love is in the air."*
- *Take a deep breath in and imagine that the love is moving into and throughout the whole of your body with this inbreath.*
- *As you breathe out, feel that you are now letting go with complete ease anything that is not love or loving to yourself.*
- *Continue to breathe this way deeply for about ten minutes or so, keeping yourself relaxed and without tensing your body.*
- *As you do so, enjoy the softness and warmth of the love vibration touching your being.*

There are no complicated ceremonies or mystical rituals for an awakening to this bigger love. However, your vibration will need to become attuned to this all-pervading supreme love through your own intention to develop spiritually. One effective way to access this higher consciousness is to raise a powerful force of energy within yourself known as the kundalini force.

Meditation: Awakening to the Universal Love

- *Get into your preferred meditation position, and look up through your third eye to make a connection to the light.*
- *Visualize radiant light rays beaming down on you.*
- *Now breathe in, and visualize a ray of light enter your body and touch your base chakra at the bottom of your spine. This light helps you awaken a powerful life force within you known as your kundalini.*
- *Breathe out gently.*
- *As you take another deep breath in, watch this energy move up from your base chakra to your sacral chakra.*
- *Now breathe out.*
- *Breathe in. Now visualize this energy move up from your sacral chakra to your solar plexus chakra.*
- *Breathe out.*
- *Breathe in again, and see the energy move up from you solar plexus chakra to your heart chakra.*
- *Breathe out.*
- *Breathe in, and feel the energy rising from your heart chakra to your throat chakra.*
- *Breathe out.*
- *Breathe in again, and move the energy up from your throat to your third eye chakra.*
- *Breathe out.*
- *Now breathe in, and visualize the energy move up from your third eye chakra to your crown chakra.*
- *Breathe out.*

Now you are going to raise your kundalini in one inbreath. Some of you may picture this kundalini movement like two light-filled serpents rising and spiraling from side to side through each of your chakras until they arrive at the crown chakra. However, if you visualize the rising movement of kundalini slightly differently, then that is fine too. Okay, let's do that now.

- *Breathe in and visualize your kundalini rise from the bottom of your spine to the top of your head.*
- *Open your eyes and breathe out.*
- *Look out into the space around you. Keep your eyelids relaxed, and focus out, as if you are not looking at anything specific.*

Take your time to just be in the here and now. What did you experience and realize from raising your kundalini and being in the present moment?

- *Continue to bring any of these good feelings into your day.*

Love Is Not Blind

Understand that love is far from being sightless. Love sees everyone and everything. In seeing all that is love, we naturally notice all that is less than love too. Many spiritual teachers and the enlightened ones have the ability to come from this stance of recognizing what is and is not love. Once you have raised your kundalini to experience the greater love — that is everywhere — you will begin to awaken to this higher consciousness within you. Love will then become your power and higher purpose.

Let in More Love

There are no boundaries to the amount of love that you can receive. The only limitations that you create are through your own restricting beliefs and patterns about love and what you believe you can have. To receive more love in your life, start by affirming to yourself that you now allow more love into your life.

As you allow more love in, not only will good things start to happen in your life, but this love will also begin to show you areas within you where there is or has been a lack of love. Life will begin to awaken you to how you think and treat yourself, how you care for yourself and others, and how others respect you. By choosing to allow more love to enter your life, you will help your heartfelt troubles and places within you that have not been appreciated, honored, and loved before come to light to be healed and positively altered to represent the love that you are. Do not be put off, as this can be a very transformative and worthwhile time; without being aware of where there is little or no love in your life, it can be difficult to change your life for the better. If you start to accept your feelings, however low they might be (and it might get a bit up and down as you come to realize everything you felt on every topic of your life), you will find yourself and your life transformed in the next six months, more or less.

For example, as you take steps to love yourself and allow more love in, you may find yourself regressing, traveling back to earlier times in your childhood where your inner child may need healing. Some of you may also start to have flashbacks to your past lives where a destructive pattern or an unconstructive thought may be rooted, which is still negatively effecting you in this present life. It is important that when you start to see images of your past — in your dreams, meditation, or other time — that you do not disregard these inner films, for they are surely telling you something very significant to help you remember, realize, and release so that you can move on to having more love.

Example Scenario

After a string of relationships with abusive men, Alison decided that she wanted this pattern to change. In her meditation time, a destructive and abusive relationship showed up as a past life. She also acknowledged that her father was uncaring and verbally abusive to her as a child. By allowing more love into her life, she realized from her wise intuition that deep down she did not feel good about herself, felt unlovable, and was afraid of getting hurt, which only contributed to attract more harmful relationships. After realizing her low self-esteem, she decided to change the way she thought about herself by telling herself every day that she loved herself and that she now allowed more love into her life than ever before. As she came to love and honor herself more and let more love in, she decided that she was no longer going to be treated this way again, and thus the pattern of damaging relationships soon ended.

Once you begin to love and recognize yourself, your relationships will come to reflect more of who you believe you are. You will soon find that those around you will either start to alter their ways to meet your new self-loving beliefs about yourself, and those who do not want to fit in with your new and positive vibration will fall away from your life to make space for new loving relationships to come in.

Nonetheless, when looking back to discover the source of your problems, try not to go pointing your finger and blaming others. There are no coincidences in this world. Remember, you may have chosen to reincarnate with certain parents or family members or to live with certain people who reflect certain beliefs that you unconsciously hold so that you can become aware of them and change them for the better.

Opening to more love will alert you to anything that is no longer serving you. For some of you, this time can be like sorting out a closet of clothes that you have accumulated over many years that no longer fit or suit the newly self-realizing you. For others, this process of letting more love in is a welcomed relief, and the transition toward the better comes with more ease and joy.

Soon enough, by letting more love in and doing the necessary practices to love yourself, you will gradually reveal more of who you really are and who you want to be. If you have trouble getting over traumas from your past, suffering from emotional pain, or feeling low, now is the time to love, nurture, and take care of yourself. There is much support and help out there in the form of alternative therapies to help you through this. Some are mentioned at the end of this step. Use this next visualization whenever you need support in letting go of anything that is not serving you and to allow more love into your life.

Visualization: Letting Go

- *Lie comfortably on the floor. If you need to, cover yourself with a natural fiber blanket to keep warm.*
- *Connect with the loving light of the spiritual sun at the third eye that is shining on you from above. Feel its warmth relaxing your whole being.*
- *Say to the light, "I now allow more love to come into my life."*

You are currently hanging on to a thought, an activity, or a relationship that is no longer serving you positively or making you feel good. If you want to experience more love in your life, realize that you will benefit positively by releasing it.

Some of you may already know what you need to let go of, so acknowledge that now. However, if you are not presently aware of what that is, that's okay. You will most likely become aware of what you are about to let go of in the next day or two after doing this visualization.

- *Picture yourself gripping firmly onto a horizontal pole while the rest of your body is hanging in the air.*

Are you ready to let go of something that is no longer serving you? Are you ready to let go of the pole? Know that when you do, there will only be more love there waiting for you.

- *Finally, you sum up the courage and let your fingers slide off the pole.*
- *See yourself falling safely onto soft cotton wool, landing gently on your*

feet, flying away into a sense of freedom, or wherever else that love takes you.

- *Feel a sense of lightness and ease, and notice the smile on your face, for you have let go of something significant that was holding you back from having more love in your life.*

A new belief rises up within you that will help you have, give, or be more love in the future. What is this new belief?

- *Put your hands over your heart and say this positive belief to yourself three times.*
- *Now open your eyes, feeling freer and lighter than before.*

Further Guidance

Use this visualization whenever you need support in letting go of anything that is not serving you and to allow more love into your life.

Release Unhealthy Attachments

There is enough love for everyone. One of the reasons that you may find it difficult to let go of anything that is not for your own well-being is that you believe there will not be anything better to take its place. But before you can receive more love, you must first let go of what is no longer serving your happiness and highest good, whether that is a negative belief that you hold, an activity that you do, or an unfulfilling job or relationship.

We are not just talking of your present-day relationships that are no longer for your joy and highest good but of relationships from the past, like old boyfriends and associations who you have not seen for years and are still energetically attached to. Stop thinking about them, talking about them, or dreaming about them. Reflecting on relationships that have long gone will stop you from living fully in the present and can even prevent you from experiencing new love. Every time you think of a past relationship, you will hook up with this person at an energetic level, magnetizing their past vibration and thoughts to you.

Visualization: Cutting Cords

This visualization helps you to disconnect from any psychic negativity that you might be experiencing from others in either a past or a present relationship.

- *Close your eyes, and go within.*
- *Imagine that you are scanning your aura.*
- *See or feel any psychic cords or hooks that are psychically attached to your body from someone else that you once knew or that you know of now.*
- *Imagine taking a pair of sharp scissors or a knife, and see yourself cutting these cords and setting yourself free of them.*
- *With peace in your heart, say farewell.*
- *See these cords disappearing forever, and sense your power and energy move back into this space.*

Smudging (burning herbs and fanning the smoke around a person's aura) while you visualize letting go of this person will also work well to help you let go of any unhealthy attachments. If necessary, carry out the meditation on the sacred heart of Jesus Christ (see step 5) to help you forgive and release any old hurts.

Before allowing new acquaintances and friends to come your way, affirm to yourself that you now allow new love and friendship into your life. New people who are a joy to be with and are for your highest good will usually smile at you, want to get to know you, and be your friend without you having to initially make too much effort.

Relationships that are happy and harmonious are ones that respect the feelings of each party and show this consideration. You do not have to waste your precious energy in rowing, as those who like confrontation usually only want their own way and like the thrill of pulling on your energy and attention.

Do not be afraid of getting hurt in relationships, either; otherwise, you could attract people who will do just that. If you love yourself, you will not get hurt by the ways of others, because you are not reliant or needy of another's validation and love. Loving yourself brings about an inner strength and detachment through which you will eventually stop worrying about what others think of you. What is most important is what *you* think of you. Then you will be a magnet for attracting people who think the same way as you think about yourself.

How could you love yourself more today? What things could you do, say, or think that would state that there is enough love for you?

Joy Is an Aspect of Love

A great joy is realized when you experience the omnipresent love of Supreme Spirit. If you ever get the chance, go to see or swim with some dolphins. Dolphins are highly evolved beings that naturally express a vibration of joy, and being in their presence can open your heart center to encounter spirit within. Joy and a childlike pleasure are just a few of the wonderful feelings you can experience from being with dolphins.

Visualization: Dolphin Joy

- *Close your eyes and relax your body.*
- *See yourself floating weightless in the waters of a tranquil sea.*

To one side of you is a scene of rolling green hills and undulating coves of white, unspoiled beaches. To the other side, a clear and calm turquoise sea stretches out to the horizon.

Through the stillness of the water, suddenly some dolphins appear. How many can you see? These dolphins have come to you with a greeting to help you open your heart and to let you know what it is like to live at a vibration of joy.

- *Let them swim nearer to you.*
- *Watch them jump and play, somersaulting in the water with great energy and ease.*

Some may even pop their heads out of the water and begin to talk.

- *Listen to the sounds they make.*

As you watch them play, a newfound joy and aliveness opens within you. Suddenly, a dolphin comes right up to you.

- *Picture his smiling mouth and look into his eyes. Instantly, you feel a deep connection between you and this dolphin.*

Dolphins are very wise and evolved creatures. This beautiful dolphin has a message or healing for you to help you open your heart and feel more joy. Receive this now.

- *Continue to spend as much time as you wish with these dolphins.*
- *When you are ready, thank the dolphins for assisting you, and bid them goodbye.*

- *Watch them joyously swim off into the distance.*

What did you experience from visualizing the dolphins? What profound insights did you receive from your dolphin? Know that you can connect with them in this way whenever you wish to experience more joy and wisdom.

Love Makes the World a Better Place

As you go about your day, increase your sense of compassion by keeping your heart open. Putting yourself in another person's shoes or remembering a time when something similar happened to you can help you be more understanding and gentle with others. Maybe that person has come home grumpy, has had a bad day at work, or has not slept well the night before. Positively empowering or helping others evolve spiritually can be considered a very high level of compassion. As you come to be more compassionate toward yourself, your empathy and understanding with others will grow.

Learn to listen. Do you butt in, turn your attention to the television, or continue to absorb yourself in playing in the latest computer game while a loved one is trying to relay something really important? Harmony within relationships is achieved by being a good listener. It is not necessary that you know all the answer; most people feel better and get perspective just by getting a problem off their chests. If you feel that you want to say something worthwhile — once you have taken the time to listen — connect with the image of light at your third eye first and then be guided by your intuition on what to say to the other person.

In the process of helping others, it is important not to take other people's problems on board. Advise and empower those who ask for help and call for a focus of light for assistance or pray. Be of practical assistance to those in need in the best way that you can, and be a light to those who ask for your help. Then let the person go resolve his or her troubles. Some of you kind and compassionate souls want so much for a friend to get well or feel better that you can take on the baggage of others as your mission, which could unbalance you or feel like a burden. Be guided by your higher self on what to say and do. Shine your light and wisdom, yet always remain detached to the outcome and problems of others.

If you find yourself helping someone discover their higher nature, you will need to develop patience and tolerance to help them through. It may all seem clear and straightforward to you how friends can let go of things that are not serving them, be more assertive, love themselves more, or break free from negative patterns, but for each person in question, it may take time to fully realize where he or she is coming from and what is needed to positively change. Again, if you are patient and tolerant with yourself as you grow, then you will most likely be this way with others.

There Is No Secret; Just Love Life

Love soothes, heals, and reunites, and it is the key to getting along with others. Miracles can happen through acts of love. If everyone came from this elevated stance of fondness and compassion, the world would be a much different and more tolerant place. Does it not feel great when someone treats you well or surprises you with friendship or affection? How could you show more love to those around you or to the planet? If you want to receive more love, then open your heart and give it freely, for what you give out, you will surely get back.

All true successes come from love, and by giving your best, you will be putting love right there. Love yourself and put love into what you are doing. Honor your family, your friends, and your community, not forgetting to nurture nature and our beautiful planet Earth. Feel your great affection for your spirit guides and the enlightened masters who are constantly there for you with wisdom and compassion, and know you are and always will be unconditionally loved by Supreme Spirit. As you appreciate life, you announce that you love yourself and Supreme Spirit!

Everything that happens to you, whether you call it good or bad, is helping you to realize more love. Whether it is to recognize the love and power within you, to be more compassionate with others, to not be a pushover, or — ultimately — to bring you closer to the love of Supreme Spirit and feel a devotion to the One, love can be seen as the higher reason and driving force behind all that happens to you. With this understanding, you can come to accept all that comes your way with more understanding, ease, and grace because deep down you will know that love is just helping you wake up to the truth that you are blessed with love.

Visualization: Awakening to the Love Within

- *Close your eyes and start to feel yourself go deep within.*
- *Take your awareness to the area of your heart chakra.*

Here you will begin to see the closed petals of a flower bud.

- *Begin to watch the petals of this bud gradually open and blossom.*
- *As the petals unfold, notice a beautiful gemstone or crystal inside it.*
- *A multicolored light radiates out from this gem.*
- *Focus on the sparkling vibrant colors here.*

In the presence of this light and color, an incredible love is now awakening within you.

- *Feel the gentle and soft vibration of love touch your heart. Your whole being is immersed in this wonderful feeling of love.*
- *Stay within this experience of love for as long as you wish.*
- *When you are ready, open your eyes, knowing that you have awakened to a new level of love.*

Further Guidance

- Every day, look into the mirror and tell yourself how much you love and believe in yourself. Speak of your good self-esteem and self-worth. Talk about the things that make you feel good about yourself and that are going well in your life.
- Affirm daily that you allow more love to come into your life.
- Practice the "love is in the air" visualization daily to help you relax and let go.
- Take a few minutes a day to breathe deeply when needed.
- Practice raising your kundalini.
- In this transformative period of opening to more love, treat yourself to some forms of alternative healing, such as shiatsu, Reiki, massage, or any others you feel attracted to. These can assist in releasing energy blocks and help you relax to find inner peace within.
- For those of you who find yourselves stuck in a rut, you may need some extra support. Talking to a spiritual healer or counselor can sometimes make things clearer. A good one will give you understanding, clarity, and constructive feedback to help you deal with your situation so that you can move on with your life in a positive manner.
- Surround yourself with caring and supportive friends.
- Do more of the things that bring you a sense of joy and self-love.
- Keep meditating on the light.

Step 9

You: a Creation and a Creator

Have you ever thought about how the universe was created and how the magical hand of Supreme Spirit goes about creating life and why? How do you create things in your life? Let's journey into the theories of great physicists and yogis to find out.

Visualization: the Creator, Creating

- *Close your eyes.*
- *Notice a spark of light in the distance.*
- *See the spark of light explode in a manner similar to what scientists today would call the Big Bang.*
- *See this explosion create a colossal diversity of creation, making up our tangible and physical universe.*
- *Watch the universe continue to expand out, getting bigger and bigger and moving at an incredible speed.*

This is the Creator, or Supreme Spirit, creating physical form. The universe stops moving outward and begins to contract, pulling in all that it created to the source where it once came from: a dot, or spark, of light.

When all creation has been gathered to that initial spark, a new explosion is created to once again rekindle life. This is the inexhaustible movement of Supreme Spirit breathing in and out, a never-ending cycle of continual creation that gives birth and reclaims all life.

- *Take a few minutes to concentrate on your breath.*

As you breathe in, you are connecting to your source within. As you breathe out, you are creating, expressing, and experiencing yourself as Spirit.

- *Continue to breathe in and out deeply.*
- *Now open your eyes.*

Supreme Spirit created all things manifest. Therefore, Spirit's intrinsic nature exists within everyone and everything. From the tiniest seed to the exquisiteness of a flower to the infinite diversity of our universe and all the living beings who inhabit it, there is no one thing or one life form that is not part of the Creator. Life can be seen as the continuous creation and expression of Supreme Spirit.

Made in the image of Supreme Spirit, each soul is an eternal expression of Supreme Spirit's love, light, and divine intelligence. The Creator made you complete and faultless — an individual embodiment of love, a reflection of godliness!

In the world of spirit, a soul only knows itself as this bliss. It shines like a star among many other soul stars. It knows itself only as beauty, love, and perfection that is at one with the Creator. Yet how can a soul really know its true identity of such goodness if everything that surrounds it is sublime? In fact, how can Supreme Spirit know of its magnificence if there is only the One and nothing else to compare itself to?

So Supreme Spirit came up with the idea to manifest a substantial and physical universe, and within that, the concept of relativity. Hot and cold, up and down, fast and slow, big and small, high and low, and good and bad — you name it — everything in our material world is evaluated through its comparison to something else. This is how we tend to define ourselves and things in our physical condition.

This great game of relativity was brought about so that each soul could have the chance to compare itself to something else, which in turn would give each soul the opportunity to see who it really is or is not. For without darkness, how can you know yourself as light? Without seeing what is not love, how can you distinguish what is?

Many on the Earth plane have forgotten their intrinsic soul nature, and that's fine because this is all part of the cosmic game. However, there are many waking up to recall. Such souls choose to evolve spiritually, and as you self-realize — that is, find out and become who you truly are — you give Supreme Spirit the opportunity to realize self through you. Thus, on a higher level, physical life was created to know, express, and experience your truth.

You Create Your Life

When you die, you return to the ecstasy of Spirit. This is a time when every soul will know the faultlessness of its spiritual nature again, at one with the One. It is then that you are given the chance to look back on your past life. Without judgment and with total detachment, you will be able to see clearly the entirety of your past lives — and even all your other lives if you so wish — each lifetime appearing like a separate but connected piece of a jigsaw that makes up a bigger picture of your continual evolution.

From this insight, you will see where you were coming from in your previous life. You will observe how you thought, how you acted, how you felt, what your motivations were, and how others felt through your actions. You will notice when you loved yourself; where you felt love, felt loved, and expressed love; where you received and gave love; and where you acted with love. You will also notice where you did not. By observing how you were in any given lifetime, you will come to see how much you resembled the honesty of your soul, giving you an accurate picture of your spiritual progress. The more love and light you are in the physical, the more spiritually evolved you have become.

Looking back in this way, your soul may then naturally want to perfect an incidence where you in the physical did not see, feel, experience, express, or act as your true self. So your soul gives itself another go, a new chance within a new life to idealize those incidences and to remember the love that it is. From there, a soul then chooses to reincarnate at a specified time, in a specific way, with certain parents, and in a particular country or planet that will give it the best chance to realize and express more of its truth.

There is no end to evolution, so there can be no conclusion to your level of enlightenment. Some may call this perfecting karma, yet karma is never a punishment in the name of any god. Supreme Spirit does not punish; Spirit only loves. But your soul, an aspect of the One, will choose to come back into life to recall and mirror any aspect of its soul self to realize its perfection a little bit more. That is why the spiritually accomplished would never judge a person for the type of life that person is living. They know that for some higher reason, souls have chosen to come into the world in expressed ways and with certain backgrounds, tendencies, and desires to jog them into remembering something about their true selves.

It has to be said, however, that reincarnation is not the only way in which an individual soul can evolve toward knowing and being its truth. Once a soul has passed away, it may go to one of the higher realms of light in the astral plane where the enlightened masters reside. Here, a soul will spend time recalling more of its truth through the help of the great ones before reincarnating again somewhere in the universe. In fact, even some of these great masters sometimes decide to reincarnate to help awaken others. Can you name any spiritual teachers who have already achieved this?

Be Wise with Your Free Will

Supreme Spirit gives every soul a free hand to choose, do, be, and create the life it wants. Nonetheless, every wise man knows that for every cause, there will be an effect, and that effect will eventually come right back to its maker, for what you sow, so you shall reap! For example, if you are looking after yourself, others, the animal kingdom, nature, and the planet unselfishly in ways that help to sustain all life harmoniously, that good will eventually come back to you through living on a planet where the weather conditions are stable, where there is no air pollution, where the food is grown chemical-free, and where there is a plentiful supply of resources for everyone. However, when your will is directed unwisely, greedily, and egocentrically in ways that will damage, harm, neglect, or even kill life, then misfortune will eventually be the backlash.

Take the issues of humanity's past and present actions to our beautiful home, planet Earth. By carelessly polluting and destroying our natural and wonderful world, nature is already boomeranging back to us the effect of our selfish and ignorant ways through changes in our weather conditions and environment that are beginning to have a devastating effect on nature and the way we live.

If humanity or any single human being thinks that they can do whatever they like to Mother Earth or to any other precious life form without feeling the consequences for those actions, then they are truly mistaken. It is the unaware of this divinely created law of cause and effect who take no accountability for their actions, and sadly, by continuing down a path of such shortsightedness, they are only bringing suffering onto themselves. Even so, this exact universal law can be our greatest blessing. With a clear outward observation of what is happening around us through our actions, cause and effect can awaken us from the misery that we create, thus helping us to understand more developed ways of being that will lead us to act in more compassionate and responsible ways with all of life.

Your Soul Has the Upper Hand

Your soul knows your agenda in this lifetime and sees the higher reason for why things happen to you and why you would choose to create something. Everything that has happened to you, and all the outer circumstances currently occurring in your life, have been and are now just perfect for you to recollect and evolve into the next bigger picture of your truth, so stop judging yourself and your life. If at present it were in your highest good to be in a different place, you would already be there. Nonetheless, some of you might feel sad or depressed that you have not yet created all that you dreamed of being or having in life. In that case, now is the time to be true to yourself and to start creating what you desire.

Be Aware of What You Think

Before you have a thought, an idea, or a concept about something, what is there? Nothing — no thing — but what can be described as an unformed energy. It is not until you begin to think something that the power of your mind immediately starts to affect this "no thing" energy to take shape, to come together into the form of what you are thinking. Therefore, it is the driving force of your thoughts and beliefs about who you think you are and how life works that go out to create your reality.

You can freely choose to think whatever you like. You can help dematerialize something in your life — get rid of it by stopping your thinking and being a certain way — or change and create something new in your life by initially thinking and acting differently. All your life and your materialized world is therefore something that you have and are, quite literally, making up!

The law of attraction states that our vibrational energy attracts other similar vibrational energy to us. Our thoughts and feelings are energy that goes out to create our reality, so if they are negative, then you will thus start to attract similar negativity into your life.

Here is an effective yet simple way to get rid of negative feelings and thoughts from long ago that are still being withheld within your energy field and only serve to attract more upset or struggle in your life today.

Regression: Transforming Negative Beliefs

You will need a piece of paper and a pen for this exercise.

- *Call on the light at your third eye.*
- *See this light envelop you, feeling a wave of inner peace wash over you.*
- *Ask the light to take you to a time in your life where you experienced an upsetting or problematic time or a past situation with a relative or friend that led you to think in a pessimistic or negative way about yourself or how life works.*
- *Let the light take you to an awareness of this time in your past.*
- *With detachment, see what happened and what others were saying.*

What negative feeling or belief did you set up for yourself when this event happened?

- *Write down the negative belief that has come into your awareness.*
- *Realize that this negative thought is not true, yet it has been and still is creating your reality.*
- *Change this old belief by creating a new and positive thought that is the opposite of your negative thought to help you create a better reality.*
- *Write this new positive thought down.*
- *Destroy the old belief, and keep the paper containing the new belief you created.*
- *Remember to read and say this new and empowering belief to yourself every day.*
- *Congratulate yourself for beginning to create a new and positive reality.*

Further Guidance

To help yourself clear out negative beliefs and renew your reality for the positive, spend some more time doing this meditation. You will be amazed at the negative feelings and thoughts that arise from old relationships, your younger years, your times at school, and some of you may even go as far back to your time in the womb or your birth, when you may have experienced negative feelings like rejection from your parents or difficulties that you had not consciously remembered before. You may not be able to change what happened, but at least you can change the thoughts that you set up around a past event, which will then help change your reality today. The more you find out about where those old unconstructive thoughts came from and then change them into new and positive outlooks, the more you will be consciously creating a new reality for yourself.

Train yourself to think positively about yourself, others, and life. Catch yourself when you start to think pessimistic thoughts and of fearful scenarios, and stop entertaining your mind with them. Stop giving them second thoughts. Soon enough, by refusing to think in such downbeat ways and turning your thoughts and beliefs into positive statements, you will be creating a more positive and happy life.

Be It and All Shall Follow

Being the way that you want to experience yourself is one of the most powerful ways to re-create yourself. For instance, if you want more patience, peace, or happiness, just start to act more patient, peaceful, and happy. Literally start to be your truth! If you continue to be a desired way — peaceful or happy, for example — your thoughts and feelings will begin to follow your actions, thus creating a whole new peaceful or happy you that then goes out to attract peaceful and happy outcomes. However, if you see yourself acting impatiently or exhibiting some other lower emotion, do not judge yourself. Just be aware of how you are being. Then let this go to the light of your higher self and you will find yourself effortlessly start to be more patient — without working on the feeling.

If you want to be wise, help others be wise. If you desire friendship, then be a good friend. If you wish to be successful, help others become a success. If you choose love, love yourself and others, for every good that you give out will return to you. This is another way to help create your highest good.

Become a Master at Creating Your Destiny

How do you make better choices? How do you know what is in your highest good to create, which will be in the best interest of everyone else, the planet, and our universe? As you meditate at the light of your third eye, connect with your wise intuition to assist you in knowing your highest good. Then act on your insights to create your heaven on earth.

Ask yourself some important questions: Who do you want to be? What is important to you in life? Some of you may find such simple questions difficult to answer at first. If so, think about who you want to be now or what is important for you to create over the next few years or so. Remember you are the creator, and if you do not like what you are creating for yourself today, you can always stop and go in a different direction. What you wanted to do ten years ago may be completely different from what you want to create today. On the other hand, some of you may have a burning dream that you have always wanted to pursue but you never tried. An important question to look at here would then be what is stopping you? Another profound question you may like to ask yourself is who are you? And if your answer is love, intelligence, joy, success, or light, what would you do or how would you be to experience yourself this way?

Once you realize your truth and know what you want to experience in life, keep yourself steadfast on that chosen track, taking appropriate action and a keeping positive attitude to get you there. Defer from changing your mind about what you want and who you want to be, as this can interfere or stop you from getting to your preferred destination. Ask the divine to help you easily release your negative beliefs, even if you are not aware of what they are. Take a good look at your beliefs about Supreme Spirit and life (both are the same thing), love, relationships, work, and success or any other area of your life, and begin to change any negative beliefs into positive ones. Use your common sense too. If you truly want to be a hairdresser, you are not going to accomplish this by getting a degree in engineering. If you choose to have a happy family, don't go around creating quarrels and always being angry at your spouse. Your actions will have to follow your desires if you are going to successfully create what you want.

How to Create and Manifest

One successful method to help you create and manifest your wishes is to cultivate inner peace. If you want to create anything for your highest good, create a sense of inner peace within you first by getting relaxed. Meditation is one way to feel calm and tranquil, as is yoga or tai chi. Running or doing some form of aerobic exercise can also be very effective in helping you lighten up, or perhaps listening to your favorite music, having a massage, or doing your most loved hobby is a better way for you to relax. One simple yet very effective way to find inner peace is to mentally relax your body.

Visualization: Relax the Body

- *Lie down and close your eyes.*
- *Take your mind down to the soles of your feet.*
- *Let go of any tension in the muscles of your toes and feet. Feel them relax completely.*
- *Let this relaxation run up your legs, knees, and thighs. Imagine any tension oozing out from your skin, and feel the weight of your legs sink into the floor.*
- *Feel this relaxation flow up through your spine, and let go of any tension in your lower back, upper back muscles, and shoulders.*
- *Feel a wave of relaxation flow down your arms, hands, and fingers.*
- *Let your eyelids relax along with all the muscles in your face.*
- *Allow your jaw and throat to relax.*
- *Continue to let this relaxation flow down through your chest area and into the rest of your torso to relax your tummy area.*
- *Take a deep breath in. As you breathe out, feel yourself completely letting go.*
- *Feel your whole body sinking into the floor.*
- *Take yourself to a beautiful place now. Let this place come into your mind.*

Maybe it is a moonlit sea with the sound of waves gently lapping onto the beach, or a rainbow-filled sky with mountains and birdsong, or a place with a sky filled with stars. Wherever you find yourself, really feel, smell, and hear the sounds of this tranquil place.

- *Feel yourself becoming carefree and at peace. You may stay and travel in this place for as long as you wish.*
- *When you are ready, come back into the room and open your eyes.*

From this space of inner peace, do you get any impulses or feelings about what you would like to create now?

Those Who Do Not Ask Do Not Get

Ask Supreme Spirit to help you bring about your desires. A good time to do so is when you connect with the light at your brow chakra in meditation. Make your request in a lighthearted or laid-back attitude, as if it is not important whether you will get what you are asking for or not. The reason for this is that if you find yourself pleading too much when you pray to Supreme Spirit for something, you could be stating that this request is hard to bring about or that you are not worthy of such good, and that can sometimes block your prayer from coming into fruition.

Once you have asked Supreme Spirit for assistance, let go of your thoughts about your request completely. Do not go over in your mind solutions, answers, or ways in which you think this request will manifest. Abstain from giving your prayer another thought, and go about your day as if you have complete faith and an open heart that everything is now being done to bring your plea to you. You can imagine yourself in a boat where the river of life is now taking you to your prayers and highest good. If you do decide to take any action to help bring about what you are asking for, go with your intuition and feelings first to know what is in your highest good. Then remember to recognize and be grateful for those signs or opportunities that begin to come your way, as being grateful will help you receive more abundance in your life.

Augment Your Trust and Faith

Some great yogis and enlightened ones can manifest the most amazing things; one of the reasons is that they have complete trust and faith that whatever they ask for, Supreme Spirit will bring it to them. It is true that your powers of creation are helped when you take action, think positively, and put your wise intuition into action. But too many of you begin to doubt that what you have asked for will come true. So instead of just praying once, you ask again and again. Well, if this is you, then you doubt in the love and power that Supreme Spirit has for you, and such uncertainties may hinder what you want coming forward. It is time to let your faith in the Creator and yourself move your mountains.

Be indifferent. Release any attachments to how your requests will come about. Be open to receiving your prayers at any time, from anyone, and from anywhere. If you ask for something specific to come through certain sources or people, you could make it more difficult for Supreme Spirit to make it happen.

To lend a hand in creating what you desire, get relaxed and let your thoughts run away with you in scenes of positive outcomes and good feelings that you imagine you will experience when your request becomes real. A really effective and easy way to help you manifest what you want is to simply thank Supreme Spirit first for what you want to happen. For example: "Thank you, Supreme Spirit, for helping me in my interview that I am going to have later today" or "Thank you, divine, for now bringing me a new place to live" or "Thank you, Spirit, for now bringing me a holiday that is in mine and my family's joy and fun." Now go on to make a request list of all those things that are now important for you to create.

How to Write a Request List

Depending on what you are asking for, some things may take more time to manifest than others. For the beginner, start with small requests like, "Thank you, Supreme Spirit, for bringing me someone who can look after my dog properly next weekend while I go away" or "Thank you, Supreme Spirit, for I now get someone to help me with the house work." What you might consider to be a bigger request — a new house, a better salary, or a new job — may or may not take more time to come about. Not that Supreme Spirit says, "Hey, that's big — I need more time," but you might need to get yourself ready to have this bigger thing come into your life so that when it finally arrives, you will be ready for it.

It could be tomorrow, next week or a year or two before you see your prayers answered from such a list, but however long that you have to wait, trust that your pleas have already been answered.

Sometimes the opposite of what you really wish for in life presents itself. Try not to despair if this appears to be happening. It might be that you are being tested to see how much you want this desired outcome, or perhaps life wants to take you in a better direction. Or it could be an old pattern or old stuff showing up that is finally moving energetically away from your life as you lighten up.

When writing a request, first say thank you to Supreme Spirit, and always use the word "now" in your affirmations, as if you already have what you are asking for. Refrain from concentrating on the negative (statements like "I do not want").

Now fill in the sentences below with your requests. There is no limit to the requests you can have come true, so make as many as you wish. Then pin up this list. For added strength, say the requests to yourself or out loud daily. Then wait and see what happens.

Thank you, Supreme Spirit, for now bringing me _______________.

Thank you, Supreme Spirit, for now helping me _______________.

Thank you, Supreme Spirit, for now _______________.

Everything that you have created, you have done so through your desires, thoughts, and actions, but these things could not have been fired into being without the original source of all creation, Supreme Spirit. In fact, there is nothing that is impossible for the wonder worker and you to create. When you are well prepared for that new step, healing, or assistance; when you are willing to think in more positive ways, act in more ways that represent how you want to be; when you believe in yourself and in Supreme Spirit; and when there is love behind your wishes, miracles can then happen.

Further Guidance

As you begin to consciously create and reform your life to be how you want it, let your intentions be the driving force behind achieving your desires and goals. As you wake up in the morning, spend a minute or so just getting clear on what sort of day you intend to have and then bring those images and positive feelings to mind. Are you going to choose to have a calm day, a joyful day, or an energetic day? Will you choose to eat less or create harmony within your relationships? The life you are going to create is always within your hands, and consciously intending to create those important outcomes in your day will keep you on track to having that successful day that you so desire. However, it has to be said that sometimes there are hiccups or things that do not always go as planned. A good reminder here is, "If at first you do not succeed, try and try again." Or put more aptly, "If you do not succeed in achieving what you intended today, then there is always tomorrow."

Step 10
Soul Reflection

Now is the time to contemplate the essence of your being, to get in touch with the nature of your soul, and to reveal the bigger picture of who you really are that will lend a hand in becoming more of your truth.

All creation is an expression of divine love/Supreme Spirit, or God. Our immense universe and everything in it — countless galaxies and stars, planet Earth that compassionately homes us, humanity (including each individual), every animal and insect, and even down to the tiniest flower, leaf, and grain of sand — is the manifestation of Supreme Spirit's love. All life is sacred.

Through reviewing creation as a demonstration of love, could you also come to see yourself as an expression of divine love? Your higher purpose in life is to be your truth so that you can express experience and know who you truly are. You will come to reflect more of your own divinity, when you have fully recalled who you are and taken action on the love, light, and wisdom that you are.

To Know Yourself Is to Know the One

Many of you still tend to see yourselves as individuals, disconnected and separate from others and the rest of nature because each one of you exists as an individual human being. The advantages of being an individual are that you are free to think, feel, and be however you choose, which will help you realize and experience certain aspects of who you are, who you are not, and who you want to be. Yet on the other side of the coin, in truth your separateness is just an illusion, a false reality that causes many of the world's troubles today. There is no disconnection between you and others, you and nature, or you and Supreme Spirit; we are, in fact, all one.

People are at their best when they are free to express their soulful nature, when their decisions and actions work toward the betterment and harmonious workings of the whole. For instance, someone might think that she is happier nurturing her own self-interests without giving a thought to how her actions could affect those around her or the planet. Whatever thoughts you have and actions you take will always affect the whole because you are, in reality, interconnected and a part of all life. In fact, what you do to others, you are actually doing to yourself because your deeds, whether highly or lesser evolved, will eventually return straight back to their maker (in other words, what goes around comes around). It takes a wise and developed person to understand and put into practice the importance that we are all one.

Try experimenting with this concept by going about your day with the idea that we are all one in mind. Do you find yourself treating others differently, perhaps with more kindness and approachability? Are you more aware of how we are treating Mother Nature? If humanity desires to live in harmony among others and in balance with our natural world, our realization of who we think we are in relation to the All definitely needs reconsidering.

As you come to experience and thus realize more about the nature of your loving soul that is unified to the rest of existence (which in essence is love too), you will come to understand that less progressive ways — such as selfishness, jealousy, hatred, greed, violence, and fear — will only separate you from your soulful nature, others, our natural world, and Supreme Spirit. It is disconnecting yourself from the world around you and from your truer nature by being any of these lesser ways that will contribute to not having lasting happiness and well-being for yourself or for the greater whole.

What pictures, ideas, and realizations come to mind when you start to realize that we are all one? How would you choose to be and what choices would you make if you were to reflect this truth right now? What things and activities would become more or less important to you in your life? Can you see how the workings and goings on of our planet would positively change to benefit the whole by living this truth?

Demonstrate Your Truth

Who are you? You are love. You are joy. You are love. The next most important question now is: Who are you now going to be?

An awakened master is self-centered — not the type that thinks too much about oneself and too little of others, but someone who is centered on being the self, including all its greater qualities. If you want to realize more of your higher nature, be more conscious of it by sharing; coming from inner peace; being serene, fair, understanding, compassionate, joyful, wise, strong, intuitive, truthful, gentle, forgiving, honest, abundant, and patient; and so on. What soul quality could you express more of to help you self-realize?

Everyone you meet is in some way helping you know yourself. In fact, we have relationships purely for this reason. For example, when someone asks you to help him or her out in some way, what this person is actually saying to you is, "Who are you now going to be?" Now, you might know yourself as being caring, compassionate, generous, or a good friend, but it is only through your actions that you will truly realize these qualities within you. Are you going to give some friendly support and advice, put your hand in your pocket and offer some financial support, or are you going to turn away and not get involved? What the other person does with your aid is, in a way, irrelevant. What matters is what you have realized about yourself through your actions. For instance, you would see that you are good, generous, or gentle because of your good, generous, or gentle actions. That is all that is needed to assist you in realizing your truth.

Nonetheless, this does not mean that you let others take you for a ride; that would be stupid, and of course, intrinsically you are not stupid. If you intuitively felt that someone was trying to rip you off or take advantage of you, you would then have to demonstrate who you were by being wise to the situation (or whatever higher attribute you felt that you needed to be) so that the person could not take advantage of you.

Many people talk about love — the love you have for another, what you are going to do in the name of love, or the love you feel for our planet — but they never actually act out their love. It is one thing to think and say a loving thought, but you will need to make your love real through your actions for your self-completion and self-realization. As you demonstrate your love and light through your actions, you will then experience your truth. The problem is that when you touch on love, the opposite known as fear can sometimes arise within you. You think, "Will I get hurt? Will I look stupid? I do not have the capability or the know-how." When your fears come in set to thwart your beautiful actions, hold them up to the image of divine light to help positively transform them.

Your Feelings Speak Your Truth

Instead of thinking your way to a solution for a problem, recognize how you feel. Your mind works to function your body and helps you to calculate and be creative, yet when you are confronted with a decision or personal dilemma, too many of you try to logically think your way around things. You become like cats chasing your tails, leaving you mentally exhausted and no further along in figuring out what to do. The mind can't and never will figure out the divine.

Your soul shows itself and communicates with you through your feelings. As you continue to connect and concentrate on your light, you will learn to come out of your mind to experience uplifting and light feelings. These sensations reflect of the nature of Supreme Spirit and your soul. Here are some of these feelings that you may come to experience while in deep relaxation or meditation. Feel free to add any your own positive experiences to the list.

- Sublime
- Bright
- Soft
- Exciting
- Joyful
- Free
- Ultimately good
- All-accepting
- Awake
- All-embracing
- Light
- Limitless
- Warm
- Alive
- Blissful
- Loving

See Your Truth with Your Own Eyes

Take some time to look at yourself in the mirror. The eyes, known as the windows to your soul, are a place where you can get in touch and experience your essence. It is here that you will be able to sense what some people would describe as softness and warmth — love — from within. However, for those of you seeing love in yourself for the first time, you may initially feel uncomfortable with this new awareness, as it can be quite overwhelming.

- *Stand in front of a large mirror.*
- *Take your time while you look into your eyes.*

  How do you feel? What do you notice about yourself?
- *Once you have touched on the deeper you through your eyes, explore the rest of your being.*

It is here that you may become aware of any outstanding qualities in yourself. Some of you could see a glow of light coming from your being, or you might see yourself appear differently.

- *Still looking at yourself in the mirror, focus out into the space around you. Some of you may detect your auras and even the presence of your spirit guides.*
- *Continue to let this experience be right and comfortable for you.*

Looking into the eyes of another can also evoke a moving and loving experience. Experiment by keeping eye contact for five minutes or longer with someone who is special to you, placing your hand on the other person's heart chakra at the same time. In doing so, you will be making a soul-to-soul connection, a deeper union that can uncover a profound feeling of love and unity.

Your Soul Is Much Bigger Than You Think

You are not just as you experience and know yourself now in this present lifetime; your soul goes back into past lives and out into future ones too. As you continue to harmonize with the vibration of love and light, what was once hidden from your consciousness may suddenly show up for you to peep into. Take what you name as past lives — it is important to be attentive to these stories of your past when they pop up in your imagination, appear in your dreams, are felt intuitively, or are perhaps stumbled on by your sixth sense as you travel to some familiar place. Realizing them can serve to help you understand, heal, and release painful issues from your past that may have contributed to holding you back from reaching your fuller potential in this lifetime. These issues can also assist you in recalling good times, realigning you to your past talents and abilities that could be beneficial for you to incorporate into this current life.

When a past life shows up, try not to ignore it. Allow it to come into focus fully so that you understand more of who you were, what you did then, and why certain things happened to you. When you are ready, you will naturally discover more about your past lives, and it is at these times that you may well find yourself being given an unexpected hand. Awakened healers and teachers may turn up on your doorstep to help reveal the concealed, or perhaps people close to you will make known their insights to you. Past-life regression may suddenly seem attractive to take part in. Be open and awake to those people who want to help you release the past and bring out the best in you. Being aware of any unhappy past life that you may have had will help to release it. Once you see it, you will feel peace in your heart as if something significant has been lifted off you.

If you can glimpse into your past, what stops you from seeing yourself somewhere in the future? And how could visiting your future self really benefit you today? Journeying into your forthcoming years can reveal insights as to why you are presently taking certain routes today. Here we are not actually fortune telling, but if you are already on a path with an intention to do or create something, then there will be a certain outcome. Your future self already knows what you can achieve in the your future, so it can broadcast back to you feelings and visions that will assist you in being more relaxed about a current situation.

For example, say you overheard that there are going to be some redundancies in your department. Instead of worrying whether you will be the next in line to lose your job, imagine that you are talking to your future self one or two years from now. Your future self will then speak back to you through your feelings and intuition about whether you will need to begin to look for another job or if you can continue to feel secure in your present post.

Linking up with your future self can bring you peace of mind and stop you from going down a not-so-favorable path. Some of you may have dreams about what is going to happen to you or other people, and this is another way in which your future self may communicate with you. Many of you have heard stories of those who somehow intuitively felt a foreboding to not get on a certain plane or train that was later seriously delayed or had an accident. These people were, in effect, linking up to and receiving feelings from their future selves on a better route to take.

The Spiritually Developed Are Farsighted

Self-aware people can slip into the greater vistas of their whole lives by recognizing certain signs that represent important stages in their lives to come. Some of you may daydream, catching visions or situations that will come about in your forthcoming years. Others may pass a building or landscape that strangely attracts or mesmerizes them, and that stays in their minds for many years, yet they have no idea why. Later on in life, you find the reason why you should be so taken in by a certain place, as you now recognize that it represents an important stage or landmark in your life today. Be awake to what your future self is trying to tell you in this special way, as it will always try to catch your attention when it is beneficial for you to know something about your years ahead.

At times, you will feel interconnected not only to your own past and future but to the pasts and futures of other souls as well. Nonetheless, be wise with your awareness. It is not necessary to tell everyone your insights; check in with your intuition to see if the person is ready to take in what you intuitively see.

As you come to realize that you are Spirit, you will be able to reach into the bigger picture of your life quite instantaneously. Then you will come to just instinctively know certain things. In fact, you are a multidimensional being, living in the past, the present, and the future all at the same time. This is because there is no time, just the one now!

Visualization: Looking into Your Future

- *Get comfortable and begin to relax.*
- *Close your eyes and feel yourself going deep within. The light and protection of the spiritual sun is now shining on you from above.*
- *Feel yourself in a space of trust and peace.*
- *Go into a corridor of time that represents all the years of your present life, from birth to death.*
- *As you look down the corridor, you can see each year of your life marked on a signpost. See that now.*
- *See yourself arriving at a part of the corridor that represents the year you are in now.*

- *Continue to look down the corridor that marks out your future years.*

What future time would you like to glimpse into? It could be one, three, five, or ten years from now. Or perhaps you would like to look into a time that will be very significant to you.

- *Decide now where you want to go.*
- *Picture yourself moving to a later date. Maybe you can see the year you are in now. See this date hanging from the ceiling of the corridor.*
- *To the side of this date, along the corridor, there is a door. Open the door and go through it.*

Where do you find yourself? What are you wearing? What do you look like? What are you doing? What feelings do you get from this time in your future? What other insights are you receiving?

This visualization helps open you up to your future to know what is coming. More insights might come to you from outside this visualization time in your dreams, through daydreaming, or from a gut feeling.

- *Ask this future self if it has any insights or advice for you that will be helpful in putting any of your present concerns about your future into perspective.*
- *When you have seen and felt all that is important for you to know right now, thank your future self for assisting you.*
- *See yourself moving back down this corridor of time to your present year.*
- *Open your eyes.*
- *Recall and make note of your insights.*

A Central Soul Lives as Many Different Selves

Your soul is a much grander being than you perhaps currently understand. A central soul can break itself up and exist as other identities in different times, places, planets, and dimensions. Your soul can be experiencing itself as an array of many diverse lives alongside the present one that you are conscious of having now. You could even, if your soul so wishes, be living this same lifetime over and over again. Déjà vu? It seems that you can appear limitless and multidimensional, yet another part of you feels so sure that you are just who you perceive yourself now in this lifetime and at this moment.

State to your higher self that you are now open and eager to understand more about your other identities and your memory will be jogged into seeing them. Movies, cartoons, and pictures will be sent to awaken you to your grander self. In doing so, you may discover new qualities about yourself in the form of hidden abilities, skills, and wisdom. Keep an open mind when discovering these other sides of yourself and have fun as your soul reveals them to you. Do not think them weird or judge them as good or bad; otherwise, you could stop yourself from fully experiencing all that these insights have to offer.

Visualization: Glimpsing into the Multidimensional You

- *Sit comfortably with your eyes shut and take some deep breaths.*
- *Each time you breathe out, feel yourself going deeper and deeper within.*
- *Take your awareness to your solar plexus area.*
- *See a golden spiral coming out of your solar plexus chakra, stretching far out into infinity and beyond, into a different time and space.*
- *Follow this spiral.*

An intricate pattern of light and color appears in front of you. This pattern can be likened to that of a colored mandala or one of those colored configurations that you create when looking through a child's kaleidoscope. Appreciate the beauty of this pattern and color.

It is the doorway where you can peep into another time and space where you also now exist. This mandala begins to fade. Where do you find yourself? Who are you? What do you look like? What are you doing? What are your skills? How do you live your life? How do you view life?

- *Take your time to explore and enjoy this other expression of you.*
- *Ask any questions that you would like to know, and receive those answers now.*
- *Now come back to your present life.*
- *Bring back any talents, skills, or wisdom from this other you that would benefit your life today.*
- *When you are ready, start to come back through the same mandala and then down through your spiral until it once again reaches the area of your solar plexus.*
- *Open your eyes, feeling enriched by this experience, and reflect on your journey.*

You Were Made in the Image of Supreme Spirit

Through your own spiritual self-discovery, you will not only come to recognize who you truly are but you will come to see this same positive light within others and their potential to be more of their soulful nature. Others may have forgotten their truth, but realizing your intrinsic good can facilitate a shift in consciousness for others to know theirs. Finally, this chapter ends with a visualization to help you reflect on an image of your beautiful soul.

Visualization: Soul Reflection

You are a three-part being — mind, body, and spirit — and you will always consist of and appear as these three parts, even when you have left your body and departed to the spirit realm. Body, mind, and spirit make up your soul's image, a divine ethereal form that can either look very similar to or somewhat different from who you are today.

- *Sit in your usual meditation posture and close your eyes.*
- *Call on the divine light of Supreme Spirit.*
- *See yourself standing in nature.*

Maybe the scene is wet and lush green as that of the emerald isle of Ireland, or fiery and arid as the pastures of central Spain, or perhaps it's a tropical place with sand, sea, and coconut trees. Wherever you find yourself, it is a very special place where you feel most happy and at home.

- *Smell the air here, feel a soft breeze on your face, and sense the ground beneath your feet. Hear the sound of birdsong and leaves softly blowing in the wind as this place touches your heart.*
- *Look up and picture the sky.*

To one side hangs the fading crescent of a new moon. To the other, the morning's sun sits radiant like a diamond against a backdrop of powder blue. In front of you, you see some water in the form of a pond, lake, or oasis. It is encircled with an array of multicolored flora and fauna.

- *Walk up to this water.*
- *Ask the radiant sun above you to reflect a vision of your soul so that you can remember more of your truth.*

Suddenly, all becomes very quiet and still. The water's surface becomes motionless to perfectly mirror the loveliness of the sky and surrounding nature.

- *Look down into the water, and see your soul reflection.*

What do you look like? Do you look more youthful, older, or different from your present self? What are you wearing? This soul image moves you deeply. Your soul reflection has something to relay or give you.

- *Receive that message now.*

The breeze picks up to gently ripple over the water's surface and rustle the leaves once more. Your soul reflection begins to fade.

- *Thank the spiritual sun for holding a focus of light around you and for revealing an image of your truth.*
- *Open your eyes and come back into the room feeling renewed and awakened.*
- *Reflect on your special experience.*

Further Guidance

- Ponder what you saw. Keep this reflection in mind in the following weeks and months ahead, as its image can help to revitalize and motivate you positively.
- You may see that you look very similar to who you are today or you might look more youthful or completely different. Do not judge your insights but allow this soul reflection to resonate with you and spiritually awaken you.
- To grasp more feelings and truth about your soul self, draw or paint your soul reflection.

Step 11
Hope from the Stars

Some of you reading this next chapter may find it rather controversial — even a bit extreme. If you feel at all uncomfortable with what is written here, then please feel free to skip it. Nevertheless, you could be missing out on some vital and far-out evolutionary assistance that is steering humanity into new and higher ways of living. However, for those of you who are open and sensitive enough to the uplifting energies that are currently circling the planet and who have a desire to evolve to greater heights, surely, you will find what is about to transpire inspirational and exciting.

There are those of you who may scoff at the idea that other intelligent life exists within our universe. Considering the vastness of the cosmos, surely we cannot be the only civilization that resides within it. A spiritual opening and transformation is gradually taking place here on Earth, and whether you are aware or not, humanity is getting a helping hand from highly evolved interplanetary life to raise our consciousness.

Your connections to your spirit guides and illuminated teachers are there to assist you in your spiritual advancement. As you are beginning to find out and as your vibration rises, you can pick up on their profound guidance intuitively and telepathically. Yet these heavenly counsellors are not the only ones who have been and are being of saintly service. There are also those who are patiently hanging around on the sidelines, waiting to be acknowledged as galactic comrades in humanity's evolutional quest, who are silently but most definitely assisting humanity in taking a quantum leap in how we think and live.

As a broadcast of light, wisdom, and love from highly developed life forms touches our domain, the consciousness of man can gradually shift to express a higher way of being, where we as a race will want to live with more joy, peace, and harmony. It is through your own ascension that you will reach a stage in which you can intuitively perceive or feel the presence of other highly intelligent life making contact here on Earth.

Visualization: Journey into the Stars

- *Get comfortable and close your eyes.*
- *A great sun shines above you. Feel that for a moment.*

Your guides, masters, and angels are now with you. They are here to send you love and protection. The space around you is being enveloped with light sent from your angels and the radiant sun above you. You are surrounded by a strong bubble of protection and light.

- *Call on a highly evolved being who works only to uplift humanity and the planet.*

This benevolent and wise being now stands in front of you. The being would like to give you a glimpse into how a highly evolved civilization lives.

- *See yourself floating into outer space within this bubble of light.*
- *Observe the vastness and wonder of the many galaxies and greater universe before you.*
- *Notice a very bright star in the distance; it's a planet!*

It is a place, many, many light-years away where a highly developed civilization dwells. The vibration of this planet begins to pull you toward it.

- *See yourself traveling faster than the speed of light toward this destination. You get closer and closer, until the planet comes into full view.*
- *Take in the beautiful color of this planet as you approach it.*
- *Touch down on its surface, feeling your feet touch the ground.*
- *Look all around you.*

What does the nature of this planet look like? Does it look similar to or different from planet Earth? What are the plants and animals like? How do you feel here? Benevolent and highly evolved beings live on this planet. What do these benevolent and highly evolved beings look like? How do you feel as you notice them? Do you know who they are or what they are called?

- *Take your time now to notice any more insights about how this civilization lives. One of these beings comes forward to greet you.*
- *Notice what this being looks like.*
- *Look into the being's eyes.*

How do you feel as you do so? This being would like to offer you some special wisdom or insight that would help you evolve and live in more harmony with Mother Earth.

- *Take your time to receive that information.*
- *Thank this special being for all that you have been shown. Know that you are welcome to travel back here whenever you wish to receive profound wisdom or further insights on how you can evolve or how they live.*
- *Bid this being a warm goodbye.*
- *Feel yourself being pulled back to Earth at a great speed within your bubble of light.*
- *You are back in your room. Open your eyes.*

Further Guidance

Sit quietly for a while and contemplate the impressions and feelings you got from being with such advanced beings. Some of you may like to draw or paint your visions. What have you learned or remembered from this journey that would benefit your life today?

These extremely developed and enlightened beings come from the outer realms and help in raising the vibration of humanity. Their civilizations have reached a pinnacle of evolution where they are skilled at living at one with each other and nature. There is much to remember and learn from our intergalactic friends.

For instance, such beings take great care and responsibility in how they think and act, and they are observant to what positively and negatively affects the well-being of all life on their planet. Such evolved beings believe and act as if there is always enough, and this means that no other being is left out or goes hungry. How many die a day on this planet from starvation?

Negative emotions that take away one's sense of well-being, such as worry, selfishness, jealousy, and the like, are also unthinkable to these beings who know that such unhelpful behavior would not only affect their positive states of mind and cause their bodily cells to degenerate and make them ill, but such harmful states can affect the welfare of those around them and their planet too. Whether it is simply cutting a single ear of corn from its stem or tenderly and patiently bringing up an offspring, all is done to honor and bring out the highest good in all life.

ET Awareness Can Quicken Your Spiritual Development

The development and happiness of humanity is very important to our caring interplanetary neighbors. Consider them as masters of life, kind and wise friends who are carefully nudging humanity to wake up to our divinity and live in more evolved ways. However, nothing is pushed or forced on us. Their method is to show us a higher way by leaving signs they quite regularly put here on Earth to lift human consciousness. Then more advanced solutions and ways of being can be realized and seeded through our own free will. Otherwise, if we actually listened to what they had to say, we might hang on to their every word as if they were gods to be adorned and worshipped, and that is not their intention.

They are known to assist in clever and playful ways like putting the odd crop circle here and there. What such strikingly magnificent and perfectly formed geometric patterns that appear in a field overnight can do is far beyond humanity's present understanding. Although, it is believed that each unique geometric pattern emits a certain vibration and higher wisdom to help raise the consciousness of humankind. The highly evolved beings sit, watching tolerantly to know who we are going to be and what we are going to do next.

As each individual realizes and holds more of the frequency of love and light, highly evolved life forms from other planets will make their existence known. Up to now, such ETs have exposed themselves physically on Earth to only a mere few. However, at present this is not the most common way that they choose to appear. You are more likely to sense them intuitively here on Earth or see clairvoyant visions of them once you have reached a certain vibration.

What types of off-planet life should you aim to make contact with? Those who are beneficial are kind and illuminated, concerned with uplifting humanity's evolution that will help to establish a new age on Earth. Deciding to make contact with any lesser intelligence from the outer realms is not recommended; out there, there are those who have the ability to read your life and your mind, but they are not here to help you or the planet in any positive way. This is not said to scare you but to educate you to what is available and to encourage you to be guarded. Also, just like when contacting the wonderful world of divas and fairies, never lose yourself or think that these life forms are better than your humanness.

Your first realizations of the true cosmic helpers will be sent in ways that you can accept. At first you may have a vivid dream in which they come to greet you; you could get intuitive images of them and where they come from in meditation, or you might just feel their lighter presence. Some of them may get very excited about saying hello for the first time. However, remember you are the one who calls the shots, so if there is anything that you do not feel at ease with, just tell them.

You will receive many good feelings and insights by recognizing these close encounters. Just one perception of these space travelers can leave you feeling inspired, at peace, and light. However, if you feel out of sorts after making contact or are aware of strange things happening in your life that you have no explanation for, then think seriously about terminating that contact. Always keep a very high standard for those you want to become aware of, because you have the opportunity of meeting some of the most enlightened teachers in the universe.

Extraterrestrial life has been assisting Earth in its evolutionary process for eons. Developed civilizations have existed in Earth's long history, and some believe that our most thriving past civilizations were helped by those who came from illuminated stars — highly developed beings who came to sow higher ways of being to assist those here on Earth to live in harmony and peace among themselves and within nature.

The Maya, the Ancient Egyptians, the Native Americans, and the Atlantean civilization are just a few of the more well-known cultures in which it is believed that highly evolved interplanetary influence could have encouraged their success. Each one of these cultures had its time of glory when an advanced wisdom was encouraged and a level of evolutional progress and spiritual awareness peaked. Looking into the times when these civilizations flourished can also awaken you to live in more harmonious ways.

Visualization: Explore a Different Time on Earth

- *Close your eyes and relax.*
- *Take a few deep breaths in and out.*
- *Feel very relaxed and light.*

You feel so light that you start to move up into the air like a balloon. Far out in our planet's atmosphere you go, until you find yourself in space.

- *Look down and appreciate the majestic blue-and-white jewel of Mother Earth beneath you.*

This journey will take you to explore a different time and civilization on Earth. You will see how the native people of this evolved culture lived. This society could be sometime in Earth's past, present, or even future.

- *Look around Earth.*
- *Find an opening leading you into a tunnel of light that will take you to a different time and culture and will awaken you to new and advanced ways of being.*
- *Descend upon Earth through this tunnel of light.*

As your feet touch the ground, you begin to see the time and civilization come into full view. Where are you? Do you recognize what time you are in? What civilization do you see yourself in? What do the people look like, and what are they wearing?

- *Let images about the way they live come to mind. Take your time to see these scenes.*

You are ready to meet someone very important and wise who lives within this culture. He or she now comes to greet you with smiles and friendship.

- *Take your time to receive some special wisdom from this person.*
- *Thank this special individual, and let the scenes from this time begin to fade.*
- *When you are ready, feel yourself being pulled up through the same tunnel of light, back out into Earth's atmosphere.*
- *See yourself descending upon Earth back to your present-day life.*
- *Become aware of your body and where you are sitting.*
- *Come back into the room, feeling fully inspired and wide-awake.*

Further Guidance

- What did you learn from glimpsing into the lives of these people?
- Were they happy and peaceful?
- What was important to the well-being and success of this culture?
- How did the people take care of each other, including the young and the old?
- How did they respect nature and honor Mother Earth?
- How did they treat the animals?
- How did they grow food? Did they share fairly with one another?
- What did you find out from meeting one of the wisest in this settlement?
- Does seeing this culture give you new insights on what we today would call primitive people?

Make notes about your journey. Some of you may even feel that you want to research further into this particular civilization.

After your acceptance of other highly intelligent life and your initial extrasensory introductions, you may want to connect with advanced beings more often because of the good vibes they bring. You may even get to the point where you experience yourself attuning with their energy more profoundly, feeling as if they are actually uniting and becoming one with you.

A soft embrace, a welcoming cool breeze on a hot day, a feeling of lightness together with an inner spaciousness, and healing love are just some of the unquestionable experiences that you can feel while merging with highly developed life and attuning with enlightened energies that can create subtle but real evolutional shifts within you. There seems to be no preference as to where or when such off-planet intelligence will touch your being; these close encounters will be felt only when you have reached a certain level of evolution yourself. Overall, their presence will make you feel peaceful, wise, light, and fully present.

Visit Mother Earth's Sacred Sites

Years ago, indigenous people of the land knew why and where to build a great pyramid, place a ring of giant stones, construct a significant holy temple, or meditate for years because of the powerful spiritual energy that is present in certain areas. Dotted all over Earth are special places where you can tap into a higher consciousness, and visiting any one of these spots or sites can help arouse the spiritual within you. Each one of these mystical locations has an opening or doorway connecting you to certain planets where highly evolved interplanetary life lives. These doorways are more commonly known as portals, and there is a significant one over the region of Tibet and one in Mexico. Mount Fuji in Japan, Peru's Machu Picchu, and Ancient Delphi in central Greece are just a few of the many and much smaller sites, and there are a lot more openings to the stars that are more or less renowned and are well worth checking out. If you are traveling to a portal area, reflect on your feelings and impressions of the place or take your time to meditate there.

Not long ago, we used to be far more observant of what was going on around us and how our actions affected the planet and the rest of humanity. For instance, by looking at the formation of the clouds or how the birds were flying, we could determine how the weather was going to be, and we knew the best time to plant and pick our fruit and vegetables to get the tastiest and juiciest crops according to the phases of the moon. Some of us still live watchful and at one with our natural environment, but many of us either have forgotten Mother Nature's laws and signs or are just too busy to notice what these observations really mean.

A higher wisdom reflected in nature needs to be remembered and lived with accordingly for the happiness and welfare of humanity and this planet. The more you commit to grow spiritually, the more you will become aware of Supreme Spirit within all life, including you. When that is personally realized, you will without a doubt begin to sense the presence of other highly intelligent life forms from outer space here on Earth. It is through their compassionate and peaceful assistance that humanity is being awakened to higher ways of being and living that will support a spiritual renaissance on Earth. We have much to thank our celestial companions for.

Visualization: Attune to a Sacred Site

- *Close your eyes.*
- *Visualize yourself sitting cross-legged in the middle of a circle of giant stones or any other special portal site that you feel attracted to.*

You could find yourself at the Great Pyramids of Giza, Machu Picchu, Stonehenge, or perhaps a place in the Himalayas.

- *Let this sacred place come to your mind now. See it vividly.*
- *Feel a special vibration of peace and an uplifting sense from this site.*
- *Look up into the sky.*

A certain star is glimmering at you. This star is actually a planet. This planet is creating a tunnel of light that comes out from itself and travels into the universe to reach Earth.

- *See this tunnel of light, also known as a portal, reaching out of Earth and going around its contour until it reaches your special site.*

The stones from this site absorb and hold important information and wisdom of the planet where highly evolved beings live. What feelings or important wisdom are you beginning to intuitively notice from being at this portal site? What information are you getting about the current state of Earth and how humanity is looking after it? What can humanity do to evolve more rapidly in this area?

What does humanity need to realize and do to live in more peace and harmony within nature and with its fellow man? What does humanity need to do to become responsible caretakers of Earth in the future? From learning these insights, what could you do personally to help take care of our precious planet?

- *Continue to enjoy soaking up the special energy of this sacred site, taking your time to receive any other important insights.*
- *Know that any time you feel the need, you may come back and visualize yourself being in this location or any other preferred sacred portal area on Earth to receive global and personal insights about how to live in more harmony and joy.*

Further Guidance

Contemplate the wisdom you received, putting any relevant insights into action that would help you look after and create a better place on Earth.

Step 12

Becoming a Lightness of Being

Every end is just an opening to a new beginning, and this closing step is a doorway through which you can move into a lightness of being if you so choose. Everything that you are thinking, doing, and being is what you are deciding moment to moment, and if you choose and intend to be lighter, you may be lighter right now through the help and suggestions laid out in this book and through the grace and love of Supreme Spirit that can come through you in a bigger way if you will just let it in. All you have to do is ask yourself: Who do I now choose to be?

Each step has been designed to help you raise your vibration to experience, and thus know, more of who you truly are:

- a unique reflection and individualization of Spirit
- an embodiment of love, joy, and light that is interconnected to the rest of all life
- a divine being

Know that there is nothing that you cannot be or do; it is just a matter of choice. Will you now see yourself in this revealing light, or will you shy away from your innate goodness only to lose yourself again? Will you let your fears drive you, or will you choose love? Supreme Spirit is within you and without you. In truth, there is only the One, a divine, sublime force of love, light, and superconsciousness that intrinsically resides within all life. Do you now choose to realize yourself as a distinct facet of this reality?

Let Supreme Spirit Work for You

Many of you think that you have to deal with your life's problems on your own, usually by thinking it all through. But there is a much easier and more effective way: Give it over to God. Practice giving over your worries, stresses, wants, and problems to the Source, and watch the wonderful and — what might seem — miraculous solutions happen.

Give Your Worries Over to Spirit

- *Put your hands in prayer position, and give thanks for the divine help that you are about to receive.*
- *Lie face down on the floor or on your bed with your arms relaxed above your head.*
- *Take some deep breaths and relax.*
- *Tell Supreme Spirit what you want.*
- *Let yourself and the issue go.*
- *Get on with your week or day knowing that God's on the case.*

Becoming your light may have seemed rather elusive, and you may have wondered when you are finally going to light up. Some of you may have felt rather disappointed in how far you have come over the years and therefore continuously put yourselves through more spiritual work, but it need not be that way. And quite truthfully, it should not be. Hard work is going against the natural higher flow of things and all can be made much easier if you let go and let your higher self now take the reins and care of your life.

Imagine Your Higher Self

- *Let an image come to mind of what your higher self would look like in the physical.*

How would you sit as your higher self?

- *Adjust your posture so that you are now sitting as your higher self.*
- *Notice the grace, wisdom, and serenity emanating from you.*
- *Feel the love, and connect with the light of your higher self.*

Your higher self would now like to show you a quality of your higher self, such as inner peace, joy, patience, or another to help you know and become more of your higher self.

- *Feel and be that attribute now.*
- *Imagine yourself as the image with the soul qualities of your higher self as you go about your day.*

For instance, if you need to reprimand your child or resolve a tricky situation, imagine light coming out of your eyes, and then speak. You will immediately notice how others react more positively when you take this stance.

As you go about your day, imagine yourself being this image or feeling of your higher self. For instance, if need to tell off your child or need to resolve a tricky situation, imagine light coming out of your eyes and then speak. You will immediately notice how others react more positively when you take this stance.

Because there is an increased amount of light now available here on Earth, the veils are lifting. That is why so many have chosen to reincarnate around this time — because there is a great opportunity to awaken with increased ease and joy. No more meditating for years on end, no more spending many lifetimes to self-realize. Your enlightenment can come about, and once attained, your awakening vibration will have an effect on your immediate family, friends, coworkers, or whoever you come into contact with in the shopping center without you necessarily having to teach or say anything. As your vibration rises to that of a lightness of being, you will be able to help others overcome obstacles and setbacks just by them being in your presence.

We think that we have to do all this spiritual work on our own! Some of you may have a spiritual teacher to guide you, and that is all well and good, but what your teacher knows that perhaps you have not realized yet is that it is only through the grace and love of Supreme Spirit, the Creator of all things manifest, that your enlightenment can be finally made real.

It has been said before that if you want to reach illumination then you must let go of everything — all the methods, all the books, all the understandings, all your old ways, and all your negative thoughts and feelings — and become an empty vessel in which your higher self can drop in and permanently settle down. Therefore, to help Supreme Spirit grace you, decide that you are going to drop everything, including all the hard work you have been doing, and give your ascension over to the One. Then stay awake and see what happens in the coming weeks and months ahead.

Once you have handed your enlightenment over to Supreme Spirit, lower vibrational feelings that you have not fully recognized within yourself before will come to the fore. All your feelings — whether they are high ones like happiness, joy, power, and self-esteem, or low ones like sadness and grief — are very important and valuable because they tell you when you are in line with or out of sync with your higher self. For example, if you become aware that you are feeling that there just is not enough, then this feeling will show you that you are some distance from being the vibration of your true self, whereas a feeling of happiness shows you how much more you are in harmony with your essence.

Some of you think that you should not feel negative feelings; you believe that you are not being spiritual enough or judge that these feelings are bad, which makes you resist the negativity you feel, go numb, or even try to override it by making yourself feel more positive and happier. You may even have felt lower vibrational feelings for so long that you think it is natural to feel this way.

But lower vibrational feelings within us will never truly lift to the higher feelings that are a natural part of our higher being until we become aware of them and accept them within ourselves. Hate, greed, fear, guilt, jealousy, depression, sadness, stress, annoyance, and feeling that you can't cope or being fed up need to be recognized within if you truly want to progress and lighten up. Then as you become aware and accept all the lower feelings, they will quite naturally and miraculously lose their heavy grip and move on up to higher feelings like acceptance, happiness, love, and — over time — even ecstasy of the bliss body, without you having to do anything. The secret to moving on up, then, is to feel!

Feel the Feeling

Initiation into a lightness of being will mean becoming aware one by one, day by day, of your lower feelings and accepting them unconditionally. An array of unrecognized lower emotions may pop up from within you as you start to enlighten, so hang in there! This could last anywhere from one month to several or more, depending on how willing you are to let yourself feel all that is low. At first, it might seem like you are on a bit of an emotional roller coaster, but this is a good sign — not a bad one — as it shows you that you are finally letting go of the old. How much you allow yourself to feel it will determine how long it takes for you to stabilize and begin to be effortlessly lighter. What may seem like a spell of bad weather of troubling emotions in the beginning will soon turn into an unclouded bright sky where peace and higher states naturally take their place, but you will have to feel the negative first.

Supreme Spirit does not judge you, so why should you? It is probably best not to act out your troubled feelings or talk or moan about them to others, although you may shed a few tears and punch a few pillows. Instead, take the emotion within and feel it fully. Some of these feelings may bring up past incidences when you felt so low. If so, let these inner movies flow through your mind but stay with the feelings. Let go of judgments of who was right and who was wrong. Give yourself some quiet time on your own, lie down on your front, take some deep breaths, and just feel the feeling until it subsides. Tell yourself what you are feeling. Ask yourself, "Where is this emotion in my body?" Then call on the light of your higher self to help you lift what you are feeling. Be gentle and kind to yourself in these moments. If you need further support, use the four-step process in step 6.

It may take a few minutes, a few hours, or perhaps a day or two (at the very most) for a low feeling to shift and move on up, but it is all worthwhile, for you will never feel troubled or powerless by this lower feeling again. You will have set yourself free.

Visualization: Emptying Out

- *Close your eyes, and see a bag in front of you.*

This bag is full of old stuff, residue that you no longer need. It contains metaphors for lower vibrational feelings, unproductive ways of thinking and being, old and unhelpful patterns and fears, and any other hidden negativity that you have accumulated over the years — and possibly lifetimes.

You have accumulated this stuff over a long time. It is heavy and has been dragging you down and slowing your progress for far too long. This bag contains things you no longer need to help you move up in vibration and to get your life flowing positively but has perhaps been hard to let go of until now. You may already realize some of these things.

Are you ready to empty out and get rid of the negative forever?

- *See yourself handing this bag over to your higher self.*
- *Feel yourself become lighter as the grace of higher self takes care of this unnecessary baggage.*

You might feel an instant release without having to work out or work on anything. It will seem as if your problems will just begin to fade from your memory. Some could experience this emptying out as realizations that come to you in the days ahead or in your dreams, so be attentive. These realizations are things that no longer serve you, and your higher self is helping you let them go.

- *Let your higher self help you gently empty out in a way that is comfortable and easy for you to handle and that is in your highest good.*
- *Place your hand over your heart, and commit to yourself that you are going to let go of anything that no longer serves you positively so that you can be more of a lightness of being.*
- *Thank your higher self for all the grace and good that has happened here today.*

As you reach new altitudes, people who once bothered you will either move up to match your vibration or move away from your life, or you will no longer care what they are like anymore. Enemies can even become friends at this level! And when your vibration really gets up, you may even look with an open heart and love at those who once hurt you and love them. Then you are free to let them go or not. Soon enough, as you work through your lower emotions you will stop thinking of your unhappy past and instead remember all the good times you've had. Resentments and grudges will begin to fall away, and only your new and bright future awaiting you becomes important.

Before long, your self-esteem will notch up, and you will naturally feel positive and powerful. Inner doubts will no longer stop you, past negativity and judgements from others will not hold you back, and you will feel worthy. You will think, "How can I make this work?" and then your higher self will tell you. Feeling better about life, you will find yourself dreaming about what you are going to create next, and you may also find yourself daydreaming about your friends and relatives in a loving way that will bring about positive outcomes for them too. Thinking this way will not be something that you will force yourself to do; it will just come naturally, and all these positive vibes will then ripple out to make positive shifts for not only yourself but for others.

Old illnesses can clear up and you will feel brighter, more energetic, more laid-back, and relaxed. One of the first signs of progression is a feeling of profound inner peace. Things that you used to strive for or that bothered you may not seem so essential now. An acceptance takes hold where life seems just fine, even if you don't have the things you wanted or have yet to realize a lifelong dream. What will become important, though, is that you are feeling up, because when you are feeling good, good things happen!

A Lightness of Being Is a Feeling

As you accept your lower feelings, your light will begin to naturally blossom and you will start to feel delicious nuances of mood. An incomparable inner peace will probably be one of the first feelings you notice. Then again, you may notice sensations of lightness (in weight), suddenly feeling you are on a natural high, happy and optimistic for no reason, unexpectedly blissed out. At first these positive feelings come and go for seconds or minutes, but over time, they will gradually increase. They are indications that you are experiencing yourself as a lightness of being.

Some other signs of your lightening up are tearing up with overwhelming love and joy or bursting into fits of giggles and ecstatic laughter for no reason. You may look out to nature and feel that you are living in heaven (which you are), feel incredibly powerful, have out-of-body experiences, encounter releasing dreams, see people you live with rapidly change for the better, have a greater awareness and knowing of who you are, or much more. Those who you are living with or in close contact with will also begin to rise up in vibration with you, and they may well show similar or different signs of ascension.

Your tastes may change, and the simplest of pleasures could become enjoyable — cuddling with a loved one, watching the birds and wind in the trees, or eating a delicious dinner. The enjoyment you get from your everyday activities will grow. Some of you may slow down or downsize while others will be propelled into new and exciting arenas to create on a large scale. Your taste in food, clothes, and where you want to live might change too. Lightness of being happens differently for each person, and these are just a few experiences you might come across. Everyone is different. Let your own experiences be unique and real.

Come to Know Samadhi

Samadhi is Sanskrit for an experience of God realization, a spiritual awakening in which a soul realizes itself at one with omnipresent Spirit. Within the experience of samadhi, an incomparable encounter of inner and outer bliss is realized. It is a place where one experiences the true everlasting joy of Supreme Spirit. Enlightened masters, saints, and all spiritually evolved souls are able to slip into this sublime state.

It is through the regular practice of moving your energy up to your third eye, being gentle and pure of heart, living in wonderment and joy, and appreciating life and the Creator that will support you in being blessed by an experience of cosmic consciousness, a happening that most definitely includes and determines a lightness of being.

Unexpected rapture! I am blessed by the purest of all delights as the veil of duality lifts while undertaking my daily duties. Without force or doing, I slip into the realm of superconsciousness.

All before me now sways and dances to the bliss of the omnipresent and ever-present love of the One. In another place, yet still quite here, heaven has come upon me.

Detached from the goings on of everyday human life, what matters in this magnificent moment is that I am with the only true reality, the unchanged wonder of I Am. And quite miraculously, all that once caused me to suffer now fades into an eternal sea of joy.

It is not unknown that, in the initial stages of lightening up, old scenarios or some of your past plays that made you feel insecure, let down, or fearful appear again. If you can see these events as just old lower vibrational stuff leaving your life, which they are, then you will not get too hung up about what is presently going on. Sit back and stay detached, because these struggles will soon fade away for good.

Once stable and on the up, your creativity and inspiration may well surge, and activities you never thought of doing may seem very attractive. You may learn new skills and test out your newfound talents. Game on!

Some of you may want to be better off financially, and of course you will be, because of the good and positive vibes that you now emit. Others of you might not care so much about your materialistic wants, but you too will see all your needs met with greater ease the lighter you are. Natural highs are signs that life is going to get more joyful and better. You may find yourself thinking or daydreaming about something, and then you will turn the corner to find it miraculously waiting for you. Things will come to work out with ease because you are now allowing your higher self to run the show.

Create Something That Brings You Joy

Why did God create life? For the sheer joy of it! Your life was created to be enjoyed. Start to do things for the pure joy of it, not because it is thought to be worthy, fashionable, or even spiritual. When you lighten up, just living and breathing feels pretty good. Moreover, when you do something that brings you joy, it allows the joy of Supreme Spirit to be realized through you.

You will come to know the innocent and happy child that you once were. Laughing and joking about yourself and life and generally being silly will come naturally to you. We can take life and ourselves too seriously, yet there is a unique sense of humor within all of us. Find yours to keep you and others on the up.

Young children will see the world as if they have never seen or tasted the fruits of it before. With awe and wonder in their eyes, everything is new and fun. Let your life take on that wow factor. As we get older, we lose that innocence and tend to take everything for granted. If you want to open your heart and lift your vibration to greater heights where bliss and God realization can be found, start to fall in love with life again as if it were the first time you saw the stars, touched a flower, or tasted a carrot! Appreciate it all. Do things that are new, fun, and exciting. Play at life like a child and nurture yourself. Be pure of heart. Visit places that you think might lift your vibration. Meditate on the light. High states can be activated this way.

Before now, you may have let your mind run amuck, have the upper hand, and share a lot of negative and fearful paraphernalia. But now the roles are going to reverse: You are going to be the boss of what you think or don't think. Your mind will be the horse and you will ride and direct it to where you want to go, not vice versa.

Just Follow Your Guidance

Encourage yourself once a day for five minutes by telling yourself how well you are doing, how wonderful your life is, and how wonderful you are. Concentrate on only the good and positive in your life to lift your vibration, especially if you have let your mind be taken over with negativity. Let this become a daily routine, like brushing your teeth. Say these things to yourself as you are going about your day or try saying them out loud in front of the mirror.

When your light lands, your mind gets quiet and peaceful and your thoughts become naturally more positive and creative without much conscious effort. If you do find negativity slipping in, then choose to either ignore it or think of the opposite — positivity.

Soaring on a new high of good feelings will naturally draw good things of the same vibration to you, such as like-minded people, better living conditions, and work that is satisfying and joyful. If you have tried to manifest something with effort before or you have given up on a heartfelt dream, watch it all come in quite effortlessly now when a lightness of being takes hold. If you still do not know what you want, then let your higher self speak and nudge you step by step to what to do and how to do it. You will be helped by inspiring thoughts and coincidences sent from your higher self once you resonate with inner peace and empty yourself of negativity. There will be no doubt about what to do — you will just need to follow the guidance and take the new opportunities that seem to pop up from nowhere.

Then there are those of you who have worked all your lives to achieve something worthwhile, bigger, or better. You have been constantly worried about how it is all going to turn out, only to find yourselves now not caring and instead accepting and enjoying what you have now. Losing interest in what seemed so important before, you will find yourself more relaxed, trusting that when a move or change is needed, it will happen.

Until you feel more on the up and stabilized, it is probably best not to make any important life decisions. Give yourself a time scale of a few months, six months, or a year to stabilize into a lightness of being (which you will recognize by how you are feeling); otherwise, you may make a decision from your old vibration, which would be something you will not like.

Once you get up, there is little going down; however, you do have freedom to choose if you want to fall asleep and struggle again. You will probably begin to find yourself so aware of how you are feeling in your day that the awareness of feeling not so comfortable will make that feeling effortlessly shift upward.

Example Scenario
Alice and Tom were having lunch. There they were contentedly munching away when Alice started to feel irritated by the noise Tom made while eating his dinner. At first, she thought, "Oh, he's really annoying me!" At one point, she could have remarked angrily at her husband for annoying her so, and perhaps this would have provoked a small tiff, but Alice turned within and said to herself softly, "I feel annoyed." This was enough to help her instantly rise up and forget what she was feeling. The couple then continued to have an enjoyable time.

If after stabilizing for a while you suddenly get surprised by a really troubling feeling, then you have probably hit a block or blind spot. Blocks are usually hard to see within yourself because either you have been running away from a feeling for a long time —a feeling that was numbed out at an early age — or you have been so used to feeling this way that it now seems quite normal. In these times, life will mirror something to you that you do not like but feel powerless to change. Those close to you can usually see it too, but no matter how much they tell you about it, you just do not fully get it. Meditate on a focus of light to help you become aware of the problem or feeling. Then feel the feeling, accept it, and it will move on up. Even the most advanced of us can do with help from time to time, so there are now powerful Focus of Light sessions available, which help you make those necessary shifts and support you in going higher. (Go to www.afocusoflight.com for more details.)

Feel before you take action. Let your soul show you the higher and more successful route through acknowledging your feelings. Then take action on your feelings, even if they seem totally unrelated to what you are asking for.

Example Scenario
Josh asked Supreme Spirit for help to get his business off the ground. Even though he was very busy accomplishing this project and did not feel he could

take time off, he started to get the feeling that he wanted to take a break and go on holiday, which seemed totally unrelated to what he was asking for. Nonetheless, he went with his feelings. On his vacation, not only did he unexpectedly meet someone who had experience and good ideas to help him start up his business, but the rest and relaxation gave him sufficient time to rethink how he was going to run his company more efficiently — things he had not considered before he went on holiday.

Before you make any decisions, whether they are relatively small like what you are going to do on your day off or much bigger life decisions, see how you feel as you begin to think about taking a certain direction. If you feel light, motivated, joyful, or abundant; have a gut feeling of positive vibes; or experience any other encouraging sensations, you have a clue that this certain direction will turn out well. On the contrary, if you feel anxious, troubled, or tired, or feel pain in your body, you will be getting signs from your higher self to look well before you leap and to be cautious. This simple yet profound way of figuring out what is in line with your light through feeling will lend a hand in keeping you on a higher path.

It's All Good News!

Your life is going to change in such wonderful ways once you let your light in. All good is on its way, and you will know it by the positive vibes you are feeling. However, there may well be some old personalities holding you back from letting go into the light — usually that last bit of control and fear. Parts of your less evolved personality may still be controlling the show, possibly because those parts like the drama of it all and do not want to let go. Also, your less awake personality may still not know what to expect as you enlighten. It may think that sitting in a cave in a state of bliss or being taken over by absolute ecstasy is how it happens, and therefore a part of you worries who is going to cook the dinner and look after the kids. Well, it could happen like that — if that is what you choose — but most of us just want to be more joyful in our lives, to feel inner peace, to create good things with ease, to enjoy life to the fullest, to have good and loving relationships, to be financially better off, to be healthier, and to deepen our connection with Supreme Spirit. In the process, we may find something special we want to accomplish. Decide now how becoming a lightness of being is going to be for you, how you want your life to go, and then tell that less evolved part of you how it is going to be.

Visualization: Initiation into a Lightness of Being

- *Take a moment or two to give thanks to Supreme Spirit for all the good that is about to take place through this lightness of being initiation.*
- *Put your hands over your heart chakra and say, "I now allow my higher self to take the lead in my life for my highest good. I choose to become a lightness of being with ease and joy that will only bring good into my life and the lives of others."*
- *See yourself in a beautiful place on Earth.*

Where are you? Notice the beauty here. Your spirit guides, enlightened masters, and angels surround you with love, joy, and celebration.

- *See them throwing rose petals over you, a sign of sweet blessings.*

You may even smell the sweet scent of roses in the air. The radiant spiritual sun is above your head. This sun's rays touch the top of your head and open your crown chakra.

- *Feel or see that now.*

The light moves down through your body, awakening your chakras. Your chakras begin to spin harmoniously to the presence of this light, each emitting its own special, vibrant color to create a beautiful rainbow that is you. This rainbow signifies emotional harmony and enlightenment. The light continues to move out into your auric field.

- *See it touching your emotional and mental body within your aura.*

A higher and finer vibration from this light helps you to awaken these bodies to a higher level of consciousness. The light travels further out, reaching other levels of your energetic being. It touches your astral, etheric, Buddha, and causal levels.

- *See a vision of you as your higher self now.*
- *Notice your divinity and your beauty. See your gentle smile and glistening eyes. You are deeply wise and compassionate.*
- *Move your posture and facial expression so that it represents this image of your higher self.*

This new and fine vibration of light is all around you now. It begins to resonate deep within you. It moves your DNA to help you create harmonious and evolved ways of being that are in line with your higher self. You are becoming your heaven on earth.

- *Feel a lightness and joy within.*
- *Thank your guides, masters, and angels graciously from your heart, for they have been with you, encouraging you every step of the way.*
- *Thank Supreme Spirit for this wonderful initiation that will in the coming days and months ahead move you to know and become more of a lightness of being.*
- *Come back into the room and open your eyes.*

Further Guidance

What positive things have already happened to you from reading this book? Write them down here. Make a list here of what you would like to see happen in your life within the next three or six months, or a year, and then give it over to God. Come back to your notes in the next few months (or a year from now) and note all the positivity that has happened to you.

Give thanks; always give thanks!

About the Author

Sarah's curiosity in personal development and spirituality started in her late teens when she became immensely interested and involved in alternative healing and mind/body/spirit subjects. By her early twenties, she qualified as a Shiatsu practitioner and practiced hands-on healing.

While in Ireland "finding herself," she was unexpectedly blessed by an experience of incredible energy she describes as the "up-most joy." This experience is known as Samadhi, which is Sanskrit for the realization of God consciousness that resides omnipresent in all life. Soon after, Sarah envisioned three spiritual masters who still guide her today. These masters prompted her to offer meditation classes and workshops on self-awakening, ultimately encouraging her to put her teachings of spiritual growth into writing: *12 Steps to a Lightness of Being.*

It never ceases to surprise Sarah how each student is positively moved and spiritually awakened through her teachings. She is eternally grateful for the work that has been put into her hands. To learn more, go to Sarah's website www.afocusoflight.com.

Tina Louise Spalding

Great Minds Speak to You

"Many in spirit look on these times of difficulty, abundance, trouble, and innovation and wish to share with you their experiences and ideas. Some famous names and faces will come to mind as you read this book, and you will glean some fine information about their own learning, their own suffering, and indeed their own experience in the life after this life, for they all wish to tell you that there is no death as you perceive it to be. They are all there in their astral forms, enjoying their continued growth, their continued expansion, and their continued joy in living."

— Ananda

Chapters Include:

- Albert Einstein
- Jerry Garcia
- Marilyn Monroe
- John Huston
- Amy Winehouse
- Princess Diana
- Elizabeth Taylor
- John and Robert Kennedy
- Michael Jackson
- Cecil B. DeMille
- Pablo Picasso
- Queen Mother Elizabeth
- George Bernard Shaw
- John Lennon
- Jesus Christ

$19.95 Softcover, 192 pp.
ISBN 978-1-62233-010-2

CD of live channelings included!

Making Love to GOD
The Path to Divine Sex

$19.95 Softcover, 416 pp.
ISBN 978-1-62233-009-6

"We are here to teach the way to divine bliss, and we know you are scared — scared to lie naked caressing your lover with rapt attention and honor. We know you are scared to kiss and kiss and connect, to feel such deep connection and pleasure that the ego starts to get very nervous, sensing the threat to the well-guarded and limited access to your heart that it deems to be safe."

— Ananda

Topics Include:

- How We Came to Misunderstand Sexual Energy
- Using Divine Sex Energy
- Specific Steps and Sensations
- Blocks to Transformation
- A Transformed View of Sex and Sexual Energy
- Following the Path to Transformation
- Reaping the Harvest

THROUGH ROBERT SHAPIRO

The Explorer Race Book 1

gives you the foundational understanding of who you are, why you are on Earth, and where you are going.

$25.00 • Softcover • 608 PP.
978-0-9293853-8-9

"Welcome to the Explorer Race — of which you are a portion. What you are about to embark on now is a way to understand the entirety of your being as well as all that is around you.

"The *Explorer Race* series — what I like to call the Explorer Race history books — is intended to give you all the background you need to understand the value, purpose, and greater vision of what you are doing here on Earth. The information contained within is intended to remind you of your true capabilities and your true capacities. Don't let anybody tell you that you have to give up God or religion to do this. You don't. These books don't take that away from you.

"These books will give you the background you need to understand why you are here and help you to appreciate your true value. The *Explorer Race* books are intended — literally — to change your life, to put meaning where there wasn't meaning before, and to provide you with the insight and wisdom you need to improve the quality of your life and the lives of those all around you — maybe even on other planets.

"That's why you exist. That's why you're here. So enjoy the liberation you feel from the wonderful insights of Book One — and the others in the series you read. Welcome to the Explorer Race!"

—Zoosh through Robert Shapiro

CHAPTERS INCLUDE:

- *Origin of the Species: a Sirian Perspective*
- *Conversation with a Zeta*
- *The ET in You: Physical Body*
- *Coming of Age in the Fourth Dimension*
- *The True Purpose of Negative Energy*
- *The White Brotherhood, Illuminati, New Dawn, and Shadow Government*
- *Fulfilling the Creator's Destiny*
- *Etheric Gene Splicing and the Neutral Particle*
- *The Third Sex: The Neutral Binding Energy*
- *The Goddess Energy: The Soul of Creation*
- *The Heritage from Early Civilizations*
- *Explorer Race Timeline*
- *The Twelfth Planet: Return of the Heart Energy*
- *Retrieving Heart Energy*
- *The Explorer Race Is Ready*
- *The Creator's Mission and the Function of the Human Race*

Tom T. Moore

THE GENTLE WAY

A SELF-HELP GUIDE FOR THOSE WHO BELIEVE IN ANGELS

This book is for all faiths and beliefs with the only requirement being a basic belief in angels. It will put you back in touch with your guardian angel or strengthen and expand the connection that you may already have. How can I promise these benefits? Because I have been using these concepts for over ten years and I can report these successes from direct knowledge and experience. But this is a self-help guide, so that means it requires your active participation.

$14.95 • 160 pp. softcover • ISBN 978-1-891824-60-9

THE GENTLE WAY II

BENEVOLENT OUTCOMES: THE STORY CONTINUES

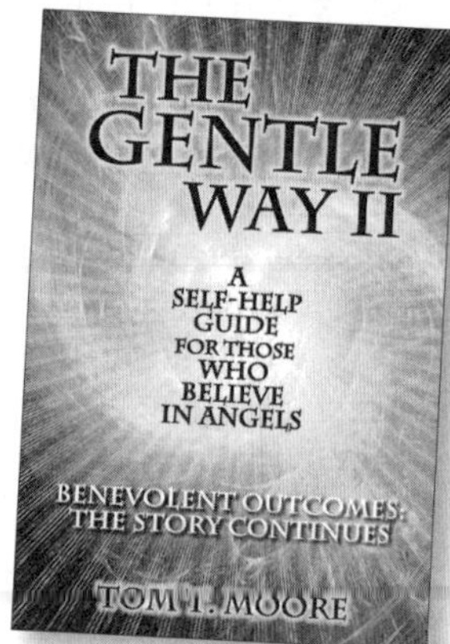

You'll be amazed at how easy it is to be in touch with guardian angels and how much assistance you can receive simply by asking. This inspirational self-help book, written for all faiths and beliefs, will explain how there is a more benevolent world that we can access, and how we can achieve this.

These very unique and incredibly simple techniques assist you in manifesting your goals easily and effortlessly for the first time. It works quickly, sometimes with immediate results — no affirmations written intentions, or changes in behavior are needed. You don't even have to believe in it for it to work!

$16.95 • 320 pp. softcover • ISBN 978-1-891824-80-7

THE GENTLE WAY III

MASTER YOUR LIFE

Almost three years have passed since *The Gentle Way II* was published. Yet as many success stories as that book contained, I have continued to receive truly unique stories from people all over the world requesting most benevolent outcomes and asking for benevolent prayers for their families, friends, other people, and other beings. It just proves that there are no limits to this modality, which is becoming a gentle movement as people discover how much better their lives are with these simple yet powerful requests.

$16.95 • 352 pp. softcover • ISBN 978-1-62233-005-8

DRUNVALO MELCHIZEDEK

THE ANCIENT SECRET OF THE FLOWER OF LIFE VOLUME 1

Once, all life in the universe knew the Flower of Life as the creation pattern, the geometrical design leading us into and out of physical existence. Then from a very high state of consciousness, we fell into darkness, the secret hidden for thousands of years, encoded in the cells of all life.

$25.00 • 240 PP. SOFTCOVER • ISBN 978-1-891824-17-3

THE ANCIENT SECRET OF THE FLOWER OF LIFE VOLUME 2

Finally, for the first time in print, Drunvalo shares the instructions for the Mer-Ka-Ba meditation, step-by-step techniques for the re-creation of the energy field of the evolved human, which is the key to ascension and the next dimensional world. If done from love, this ancient process of breathing prana opens up for us a world of tantalizing possibility in this dimension, from protective powers to the healing of oneself, of others, and even of the planet.

$25.00 • 272 PP. SOFTCOVER • ISBN 978-1-891824-21-0

LIVING IN THE HEART

Includes Heart Meditation CD

"Long ago we humans used a form of communication and sensing that did not involve the brain in any way; rather, it came from a sacred place within our hearts. What good would it do to find this place again in a world where the greatest religion is science and the logic of the mind? Don't I know this world where emotions and feelings are second-class citizens? Yes, I do. But my teachers have asked me to remind you who you really are. You are more than a human being, much more. For within your heart is a place, a sacred place, where the world can literally be remade through conscious cocreation. If you give me permission, I will show you what has been shown to me." —Drunvalo Melchizedek

$25.00 • 144 PP. SOFTCOVER • ISBN 978-1-891824-43-2

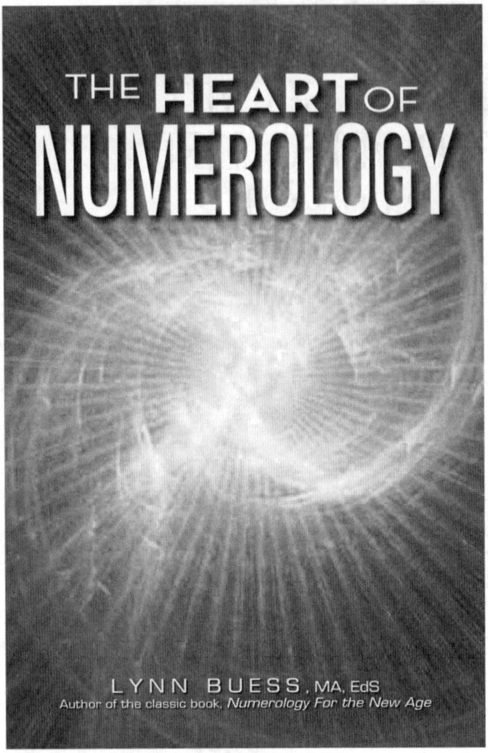

THE HEART OF NUMEROLOGY

by Lynn Buess

Numerology is a symbolic study of rhythms, cycles, and vibrations. In its most esoteric form, numerology simply reflects the tides and cycles of creation as set in motion by the Creator. As it is more commonly practiced, numerology provides a means of understanding cyclical patterns or qualities related specifically to your personal life. By understanding your own particular rhythm, it becomes easier to flow with life. Through the study of numerology, you can become more attuned to your own permanent atom and realign with the dance of the cosmos. With such understanding, you can become the master of fate rather than a victim of destiny's circumstances.

Chapters Include:

- The Big Four Primary Numbers
- The Symbolism of Numbers
- The Progressed Life Chart
- Name Changes
- The Karmic Lessons of Numbers
- Release Negative Patterns

$25.30 Plus Shipping
ISBN 978-1-891824-97-5
Softcover • 512 PP.
6 x 9 Perfect Bound

Other books by Lynn Buess:

Forever Numerology
ISBN 978-1-891824-65-4
Softcover • 320 PP.
$17.95 plus shipping

Numerology for the New Age
ISBN 978-0-929385-31-0
Softcover • 262 PP.
$11.00 plus shipping

Numerology: Nuances in Relationships
ISBN 978-0-929385-83-7
Softcover • 352 PP.
$13.75 plus shipping

Print books: visit our online bookstore www.LightTechnology.com
eBooks available on Amazon, Apple iTunes, Google Play, and Barnes & Noble

Light Technology PUBLISHING

SEDONA Journal of EMERGENCE!

ORDER ONLINE!
SAVE expensive freight or postage on your *Sedona Journal* subscription

ORDER NOW!

TO RECEIVE SPECTACULAR SAVINGS!

We are now making ELECTRONIC SUBSCRIPTIONS

available for the *Sedona Journal of Emergence!*
We have now added content that will not fit into the printed magazine!

- Get the entire journal online by subscription — and get it 2 weeks before it goes on the newsstand!
- Save on expensive freight or postage on your *Sedona Journal* subscription!

Electronic Subscriptions

❒ 1 yr. . . . .$29 ❒ 2 yrs. $55

All Electronic and Combo Subscriptions *MUST* be purchased online at: *www.sedonajournal.com* to obtain username and password

---

Get the Best of Both Worlds! Special Combo Offers!

U.S.A.

Get BOTH Printed AND Electronic Subscription - U.S.A. only

1st Class ❒ 1 yr. . . $82 ❒ 2 yrs. . . $159
2nd Class ❒ 1 yr. . . $59 ❒ 2 yrs. . . $109

Canada & Mexico

Get an Airmail Printed Subscription Along with an Electronic Subscription for Only

❒ 1 yr. . . . $95 ❒ 2 yrs. . . . $179

NOTE: The U.S. Postal Service has changed postal rates, eliminating Canadian and global 2nd Class Surface and increasing all airmail rates.

All Countries

Except U.S.A., Canada, & Mexico

Get an Airmail Printed Subscription Along with an Electronic Subscription for Only

❒ 1 yr. . . . $152 ❒ 2 yrs. . . . $285

NOTE: The U.S. Postal Service has changed postal rates, eliminating Canadian and global 2nd Class Surface and increasing all airmail rates.

---

yes! *Send Me:*

USA Printed and Mailed Subcriptions

1ST CLASS	2ND CLASS
❒ 2 yrs $129	❒ 2 yrs $79
❒ 1 yr $65	❒ 1 yr $43

CANADA & MEXICO

AIR
❒ 2 yrs (24 issues)............ $149
❒ 1 yr (12 issues) $79
U.S. dollars only

NOTE: The U.S. Postal Service has changed postal rates, eliminating Canadian and global 2nd Class Surface and increasing all airmail rates.

ALL COUNTRIES Except USA, Canada & Mexico

AIR
❒ 2 yrs (24 issues)............ $255
❒ 1 yr (12 issues) $136
U.S. dollars only

NOTE: The U.S. Postal Service has changed postal rates, eliminating Canadian and global 2nd Class Surface and increasing all airmail rates.

Name: ______________________________

Address: ______________________________

City: ______________ State: ________ Zip: ________

Phone: ______________ Email: ______________

Gift Recipient Name: ______________________________

Address: ______________________________

City: ______________ State: ________ Zip: ________

Personalized Gift Card from: ______________________________

METHOD OF PAYMENT:

❒ CHECK ❒ M.O.

❒ VISA ❒ MASTERCARD ❒ DISCOVER ❒ AMEX

CARD NO. ______________________________

EXPIRATION DATE ______________________________

SIGNATURE ______________________________

Phone: 928-526-1345 or 1-800-450-0985 • Fax: 928-714-1132

Light Technology PUBLISHING

EASY ORDER 24 HOURS A DAY

1 Order ONLINE!
www.lighttechnology.com

Email:
customersrv@
lighttechnology.net

www.LightTechnology.com
Shopping Cart w/ Secure Transactions
In-Depth Information on Books, Including Excerpts and Contents
Use Our Great Links to Other Sites

2 Order by Mail
Send To:
Light Technology Publishing
PO Box 3540
Flagstaff, AZ 86003

SEDONA
Journal of EMERGENCE!

www.SedonaJournal.com
Read Excerpts of Monthly Channeling and Predictions in Advance
Use Our Email Links to Contact Us or Send a Submission
Electronic Subscriptions Available — with or without Print Copies

3 Order by Phone
800-450-0985
928-526-1345

DOWNLOAD THE BOOK FOR FREE
BENEVOLENT MAGIC
& Living Prayer
Ancient Secrets of Feminine Science

www.BenevolentMagic.com
Learn the techniques of benevolence toward self and benevolence toward others and you will create global peace. Download all the techniques of benevolent magic and living prayer for FREE!

4 Order by Fax
928-714-1132

www.ExplorerRace.com
All of humanity constitutes the Explorer Race, volunteers for a grand and glorious experiment. Discover your purpose, your history, and your future. Download the first chapter of each book for FREE!

Available from your favorite bookstore or:

LIGHT Technology PUBLISHING

MasterCard VISA AMERICAN EXPRESS DISCOVER PayPal

www.ShamanicSecrets.com
What we call shamanism is the natural way of life for beings on other planets. Learn to be aware of your natural self and your natural talents and abilities. Download the first chapter of each book for FREE!

Print books: visit our online bookstore www.LightTechnology.com
eBooks available on Amazon, Apple iTunes, Google Play, and Barnes & Noble